Life
STORIES

CW01465825

Protected by Feathers
Encircled by Rainbows

Day One

© Day One Publications 2022

ISBN 978-1-84625-737-7

British Library Cataloguing in Publication Data available

Published by Day One Publications
Ryelands Road, Leominster, HR6 8NZ
Telephone 01568 613 740
North America Toll Free 888 329 6630
email—sales@dayone.co.uk
web site—www.dayone.co.uk

The front cover image and the line drawings throughout this book are
© Karen Coulthard

Printed by 4edge Limited

Contents

Foreword

Way back about 1000 years BC, King Solomon expressed the view that 'of the making of many books there is no end', perhaps not realising that he himself was making a notable addition to the available list. At the end of that era, Doctor Luke begins his first book, by remarking on how many people had taken up their pens to record the impact that Jesus Christ was having on their world at that time. Because he had been there and seen it all, it 'seemed good to him also to write an orderly account', and we are grateful for his Gospel and the book of Acts to this day. Fast forward another 2000 years and it seems the urge to rush into print is as strong as ever. Be it 'celebrity', politician, sports-person—and Royal even—they are all at it! Not so the author of this volume, Eunice Nevey.

As a missionary nurse in Congo for a number of years, nursing sister and carer in the UK, Eunice took some persuasion to take this step. When others were putting together a programme for a church social or testimony meeting, or filling a 'slot' at all sorts of gatherings, she could be relied upon to willingly share a story of her experience of God's care and guidance. She would deliver these from a written script in a clear voice, which would draw the listener into the story and bring it to life. Eventually these 'spots' became a regular feature at her church's fortnightly Friday 'Connect' meeting, with each episode ending in a 'cliff-hanger' and a tantalising 'I'll tell you what happened, next time' from Eunice. That is when the persuasion began!

Happily, the persuasion worked and we now have *Protected by Feathers, Encircled by Rainbows*. It is a record of an ordinary life committed to God, lived to the full, and used by Him for the blessing of others.

I will enjoy reading it, and I am sure you will too.

Ray Walker
Halesowen, August 2021

Thanks and Acknowledgements

What would possess an elderly woman in her early eighties to use the time of lockdown, brought upon us by the Coronavirus pandemic, to get out pencil and paper to write her life story? I have asked myself this question numerous times over these past months.

My life, I suppose, has not been an ordinary 'run of the mill' life by any stretch of the imagination. It is not all that many people who have had four mothers, for example, or been hugged by a massive bird, or been encircled by a rainbow—or Brocken spectre, to use the correct term. This phenomenon, I understand, is caused when sunlight reflects off the clouds below a rainbow in certain weather conditions.

Before I left Africa for the last time in 1984, the words leaping off the page of my Bible were from Mark's Gospel, Chapter 5, verse 19: 'Go home and tell what God has done for you.' I could be in no doubt that God was using that word to speak to me, telling me that my time in that beautiful land was over. I did not want to leave, but circumstances became untenable and I had to obey. After this introduction, I have included a poem that I wrote a few years ago, which I decided to include as it fits in so well with my story.

That word, however, stayed with me, and on my return home, being asked to lead the 'Ladies Leisure Hour' at my home church and to speak at various meetings in the district and further afield, I used these opportunities to obey God's word to me.

As time has gone on, owing to family commitments, others have carried on and the Ladies Leisure Hour has become 'Connect' and is open to men as well. It was at this meeting during the months prior to lockdown that I had been sharing a portion of my story and leaving my listeners each time 'on a knife edge' wondering what was going to happen next.

It was, I believe, at the last meeting prior to lockdown that one listener came to me and said, 'You will have to write that down, it must not be lost.' As I prayed over this, I realised that this could be another way of 'telling what God had done for me'. So thank you, Mr Raymond Walker, for putting the seed thought into my head and writing such a beautiful foreword for my book. He and so many others have been such an inspiration and encouragement to me. Thank you everyone.

My grateful thanks also goes to Mr M Prest, the Director of UFM Worldwide for giving me permission to use the Mission's name, and to all the office staff who have been most helpful.

This book would never have been printed without the amazing help and encouragement of Mrs Cherrill Mason, who so kindly offered to type the manuscript for me. It needed ingenuity to do this during lockdown (we had to stay in our own homes because of the danger of catching the Coronavirus). So we found ourselves dictating and typing long distance, my reading the script over the phone and Cherrill typing furiously, taking advantage of the 'free time' we were allowed by our suppliers. It took a while, but we got there. Her help and advice have been invaluable in so many ways. I could not have done it without her help.

My sincere thanks also to Mrs Karen Coulthard for the beautiful, humorous sketches which I hope will make you chuckle as much as they did me. Thanks Karen, you have done a wonderful job.

Also, my grateful thanks goes to Mr and Mrs Ian Thornley for coming to my rescue so many times over computer problems, for

Thanks and Acknowledgements

proof-reading, advice, and making a paper copy of the script which was so helpful and much easier for me to see than on a computer screen. Their help and advice have been invaluable.

My gratitude is also extended to my family, my brother-in-law Mr Reginald Wall and my niece, Miss Melonie Wall, to my church family and Mission family, and to friends, neighbours and acquaintances for all their encouragement to keep going over the past months.

However, first and foremost my very sincere thanks to God, my heavenly Father, who has given me the most amazing life and the memory to retain so well the things that I have been able to recount. Also for His grace, care and kindness over all of my life, and for leading me to salvation through the Lord Jesus Christ by the power of God the Holy Spirit when I was only eleven years old.

Eunice Nevey
Kidderminster, September 2021

The Maniac of Gadara

A frenzied shriek pierced thro' the heavy, humid air.
Wary faces hurry by, knowing to beware.
Figure wild, unclothed, untamed, in the falling gloom,
Took a stone to cut himself, crouched beside a tomb.

His darting eyes searched thro' the quickly fading light,
As burning day gave way to blessed cool of night.
Face contorting, dark with the evil spirits' power,
Who reigned supreme within him in that hour.

But, far across the lake, a man was standing tall,
While walking in the cooling foam, He heard a call.
His gaze was steady, His face wore a kindly air.
He saw that man who lived among the gravestones there.

So, gathering up His friends, He got into the boat
and in the chill night air, He pulled round him His coat.
Soon each one was riding the heavy swelling tide,
to get to that poor creature on the other side.

But, back in the graveyard, the man saw them coming,
He watched them intently, before he came running
with short, darting movements, for he wanted to see
them all land on the beach, under that old olive tree.

Once again he shrieked, followed by a long, low moan,
his fingers clutching fiercely, round the now sharp stone,
which he used to cut himself, 'til his blood ran red.
His wrist still held the chain, by which he'd once been led.

Broken them clean off, he had, snapped them like a twig.
Each link so strong and sturdy, each one so very big.
Nothing strong enough was found, that could ever tame
this Maniac of Gadara, whom Satan did claim.

Dirty, matted, tangled hair, almost hid his face.
O'er his filthy, dirt-grimed skin, one could hardly trace
a part unscarred, cut by stones, pain he didn't feel.
Spittle dripped from jabbering lips. On one knee did kneel.

Watching for that little boat, as it nearer drew.
Somehow, somewhere deep inside, it's as if he knew
there was One within that bark, who could set him free,
from those awful powers that bound, bring him liberty.

Watched he Him, as He approached, in the graveyard there.
Fear gripped his tortured spirit, mingled with despair.
Jerkily he moved towards Him and, in spite of fear,
Looked into a face so loving, saw a falling tear.

Bending low before that One, looked up to His face.
Saw such love and tenderness, wondered at the grace.
Heard Him speaking 'What's your name?' 'Legion', he replied,
'Come out right now,' He said, 'foul spirits there inside.'

Upon a hillside near a herd of swine did feed,
And into them the demons fled at lightning speed.
With hideous shrieks the pigs raced down the hillside steep,
And in the inky waters drowned within the deep.

But those who kept the pigs were filled with dreadful fear.
Off they raced into the town, telling far and near
What had happened to their pigs and the man possessed,
How their livelihood was gone and the maniac blessed.

Many hurried out that night, from their village mean,
Wondering what might meet their gaze at that graveyard scene.
Saw the man, now whole and sane, sitting at the feet
of the Saviour, washed and clean, dressed in clothing neat.

Fear gripped them, anger too; hostile grew the crowd.
'Go away! We don't want you,' voices raised aloud.
Looking then into each face, sadness filled His heart,
Seeing there the darkness deepen, turned He to depart.

As He went He was aware of one at His side:
'Master, take me with you, please?' so the healed man cried.
'No, go home! Tell what God has done for you,' said He.
Stepped He then into the boat, by the olive tree.

Casting demons out today, by His awesome power,
Pride and selfishness and fear, each foul one must cower.
For He longs to make you whole, healed in your spirit,
At his feet, clean and clothed, true Life to inherit.

🔹 Meet the family

Big tears welled up in the grandmother's eyes and a strangled sob caught in her throat. She gazed at the tiny blue lifeless form that the midwife was desperately trying to make breathe. Why did they live in such an isolated place? It was no use sending for a doctor, one would not arrive in time. Nothing seemed to have any effect, and as the mother was in need of her help she gently laid the baby in the drawer, taken from the chest of drawers that had been prepared to receive the newborn child. Satisfied that the mother was comfortable, the midwife turned to look at the infant—her eyes widened in astonishment at what she saw. The baby, who was so tiny that she could fit into a pint sized jug, was a lovely pink colour and sleeping peacefully.

With her work completed and happy that all was satisfactory, she prepared to leave the mother and her newborn daughter. Walking down the garden path, bordered on both sides with richly perfumed roses and other cottage garden delights, she went through the gate and on to the riverside path. This took her back to the nearest town of Bewdley, for that, or a path through the Wyre Forest, was the only means of access to the property.

Claypit Cottage nestled cosily into the wooded bank that rose sharply up at the rear of the

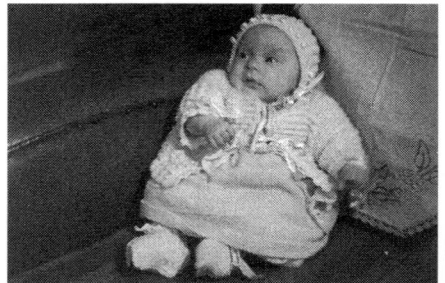

Baby Eunice

property, as it watched over the softly flowing waters of the River Severn on that warm, end-of-summer day in late September, 1938. For, so it was in this beautiful, idyllic spot that I was born.

The first years of my life were spent at Claypit Cottage with my Dad Harry, a forestry worker who normally felled timber and did other arboreal work, but at this time busied himself making pit props for use in the coal mines, doing his bit helping with the war effort. Owing to his poor eyesight he was exempt from front line duty in the war that was raging at that time. My mom, Annie, but always called Nance, was battling with tuberculosis, which we believe she caught while caring for her sister who sadly died from the disease. The only other adult living at Claypit Cottage was my Granma, Louisa, who had come to help out while Mom was ill.

My sister Beryl was seven years old when I was born and did not take kindly to sharing some of the attention she was used to receiving before I came along. She always wanted to go off and play, do her own thing, not stay to help out or rock my pram when I was crying.

Mum, Dad and sister Beryl on Motorbike at Claypit Cottage which was sadly destroyed by fire some years later—now rebuilt

One day she was given this task when the family were very busy, but she wanted to play in the tent Dad had put up for her in the orchard. She was not happy and put a large amount of angry energy into her task and gave one great, big push, and the handle of the pram with me in it slipped from her fingers, racing down the sloping path. The gate was wide open and she watched in horror as I sped through it, out onto the riverside path and heading swiftly for the river. However, Dad saw what was happening and, running as fast as he could, just managed to grab the pram's handle as it was about to hit the water, saving him and me from drowning, as he couldn't swim! My sister? She didn't hang around. When it came to teatime, though, she sheepishly appeared. She wasn't going to miss her tea!

During the better weather we had many visitors as fishermen, and often their families, came to buy jugs of steaming hot tea, sandwiches and cake as they enjoyed their sport. Many of our family members and friends came too, as it was a delightful spot for a day out.

However, it was not the easiest place to live as all the groceries had to be carried along the riverside from the nearest town of Bewdley.

The kettle was always kept busy as water was boiled over the fire to make the numerous jugs of tea, and the oven was kept hot for baking cakes to include with the sandwiches. There were no modern conveniences either—our water was from a pump situated over the well on the yard and we collected firewood from Wyre Forest to heat the water for the tea and to cook our food on the old range. Oil lamps and candles gave us light.

We washed ourselves in the sink in the kitchen and bathed in an old galvanised bath put in front of the fire each Saturday evening, heating the water in the boiler intended for boiling the washing, for there was no bathroom. The toilet was a bucket in a shed a little distance from the house in the orchard.

However, the winters were very hard and we were snowbound for weeks at a time. Flooding was also a problem, the property being so close to the river. When this happened, the family would move upstairs and the only way to leave or enter the property was by crawling along a plank of wood from the bedroom window to the wooded hillside that rose sharply up at the back of the house.

When this happened, water had to be carried from a pipe Dad had laid from a spring some distance from the house, in the forest.

There it was I lived with my parents, my sister, and my Granma. Life was hard for the family, as my father's work in the Wyre Forest was poorly paid as the house went with the job. The café-type work helped to generate a little more income.

My mother's condition was worsening and it was impossible for us to visit her when she went into a sanatorium, living in such an isolated place. So the time was brief that I spent in that lovely old cottage beside the river, and we moved into the town of Kidderminster.

My mother being unable to care for me, it meant that I was brought up by my grandmother who kindly and gladly took over the role. I was to her 'the little daughter she always longed for but never had'. As I grew, she sat each afternoon on the couch with me and taught me the alphabet and numbers. We sang nursery rhymes together and read simple stories, like Peter Rabbit, the Tale of Johnny Town Mouse and Jemima Puddle-Duck, instilling in me a love of reading. Each night she taught me to say a prayer when I got into bed.

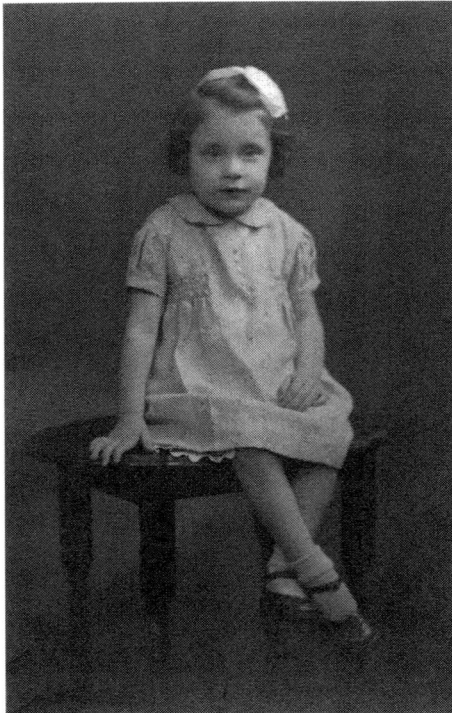

Eunice, aged about 4

Gentle Jesus, meek and mild,
Look upon a little child;
Pity my simplicity,
Suffer me to come to Thee.

However, I didn't hear right and found I was praying for some mice in a place called Plicity! It took me a while to realise my mistake! God must have had a chuckle every time He heard me. I believe He did hear me, and answered my prayer.

As time went on, Granma taught me to knit, crochet, embroider, make wool and rag rugs, patch, darn socks and hem stitch. I will always be grateful to her for all her love and kindness to me. Her ways were very old-fashioned, however, and I often felt different from other children. I was sent to school wearing a pinafore, the only child in the school to do so, and I had to wear a red pixie hat all the time, winter and summer, as I often had sore throats and ear problems. Poor Granma never understood why the ties grew longer and longer. I never let on that I often took it off and used it as a skipping rope from time to time!

How different this move into Kidderminster proved to be for my sister and myself. We now had other children to play with, but with them mostly being my sister's age I felt rather left out and found myself on the sidelines, watching the others play. How worried I was when they did things that I felt they should not be doing, or were dangerous. Things like jumping on to the backs of some horses in a field, and being thrown as the animals bucked and reared in an effort to dislodge them, then running for their lives as the huge beasts turned on them.

One very hot summer's day, we were playing together swinging on a large branch of one of a group of beautiful trees. Quite a number of us were there, dressed only in our bathing suits but with me also in the detestable red pixie hat! We were so intent on our play that we did not notice the darkening sky, until a thunder bolt struck the tree next to the one we were playing on, splitting it in two and setting it on fire. Then, as we stood there staring at the tree, the rain started to pour down in torrents. The boy who had been swinging on the branch at the moment the tree was struck, fell off into the stinging nettles underneath.

Chapter 1

My sister grabbed me and started to run with me tucked under her arm, until we arrived at some nearby houses that had covered entrances and we ran to shelter in one of them. The others soon joined us, but the lady of the house was not at all happy to have us sheltering in her entrance, and shaking her broom at us ordered us off! Needless to say, we didn't budge until our fathers came for us with our coats and took us home.

I was six years old when my mother lost her battle with pulmonary tuberculosis, and because I was a frail, sickly child, my father felt that country air was what I needed and we moved again into the country. Several cottages were situated around a lovely grassy area called Pound Green, which was bordered by beautiful mature cherry trees. It was into one of these that Dad, Granma and I moved. My sister was by now starting her working life and went to live in at the farm where she worked.

The cottage we moved into was tumbling down, with the sky showing clearly through the large crack in the bedroom ceiling, through which several stars were quite visibly twinkling on a clear night.

Again, there were no modern conveniences at all. We cooked on an old fashioned range using wood, which Granma used to collect from the forest every day. It was sawn into logs in the big old woodshed that was part of the property and that sat adjacent to the scullery. An Aladdin paraffin lamp provided light in the living room but candles were used elsewhere. The shadows these produced were very frightening to a six year old child.

My job was to wash up after the evening meal, in the scullery, which was situated at the far end of the house. A dark empty room lay between me and the sitting room where the others were, and a candle was needed on darker evenings, which flickered terribly and was in danger of being blown out in the draughty cottage. Hot water from the kettle was poured into a bowl for me and I had only a bar of Sunlight soap to make suds with. These were soon gone with all the grease of the meal. I did like to play a little with the bubbles, so the water went cold very quickly, especially on colder evenings.

Most evenings the meal was thick slices of very fat bacon or ham accompanied by potatoes and spring greens or purple sprouting from the garden. I could have managed to cope with that, but it was the fat that came from the meat that was poured over the meal in place of gravy, that saw me eating practically none of it. Most nights there was usually a colander to wash and the saucepan the greens were cooked in. The greens would be dried fast to them both and I was often called back to wash them again as they were not clean! I grew to hate greens and colanders!

It was a very draughty house, and the candle would flicker dreadfully and I was terrified it would go out and leave me in the dark while washing up. Behind me was the door to the wood shed and I could hear the rats in there as I worked. One night it got too much when I glanced over my shoulder and saw a big rat squeezing itself through the hole in the door to join me in the kitchen. I screamed and help wasn't long in coming, but I still had to finish the washing up!

The property was infested with vermin, so we set traps around where we sat by the fire at night and could catch up to ten mice and rats each evening as we sat listening to the radio!

The toilet was again a bucket in a shed in the garden, and if a visit was needed after dark I was given a lit candle in a jam jar to show me the way. How I guarded it on windy nights, for I was fearful that it would go out and leave me in the dark! There were two things that terrified me: one was the dark and the other was the spiders that lurked in that little house, or anywhere else for that matter. A visit after dark was usually a very quick affair and certainly an ordeal!

I hated having to go to bed at night during the winter months because it was so cold and so dark. At 7 pm each evening I was made to put away whatever I was doing and go upstairs to bed. I put forth every excuse in the book not to go, but it was no use, they always won in the end! Granma always came upstairs with me and grumbled at me for dawdling. I got into bed and pulled the bedclothes up so that only my eyes were showing. Taking the candle with her, she went back to her knitting downstairs, leaving a very frightened little girl peering around the dark room. My eyes fixed on the wardrobe from where I was sure some monster would suddenly leap out and get me!

Then it was the large picture on the wall before me. It was an advertisement for Sunlight Soap, I have since realised, and so the enhanced whiteness of the people's clothes really showed up in the dark room. It was of some elderly ladies standing to admire a little child sat on its mother's lap. They were mostly dressed in white, which shone. There was an elderly lady with her walking stick, and as I stared at the picture this old lady lifted the stick and hit the child on the head. I was terrified that she would come and hit me next! After staring for some time I plucked up courage and pulled the bedclothes over my head and lay there shaking! No beast ever came out of the wardrobe and I was never hit on the head with the old lady's stick. How irrational are our fears, but oh! so real at the time!

Our water came from a well in the cellar which supplied us with good, cold, refreshing water, but often in winter the place was flooded and one returned with wet feet. It was dark and again infested with vermin and spiders. Steep stone steps led down to the floor level and I was not allowed in the cellar, for which I was very thankful. In the summer this supply dried up completely and then we had to collect water from a spring in the ditch at the side of the road that ran past the property!

There was a fairly big garden, which was put to good use growing our own vegetables. We kept chickens and a pig, and cherry trees grew around the green just outside the property. How we enjoyed this delicious fruit each year! Perhaps that was where my love of growing things was nurtured, for I was delighted to have a special little plot for my own use. How well I remember breaking the heads off the flowers in the garden and planting them in my plot. Oh the disappointment when evening came and I found they had all withered and died!

Granma gave me seeds that she had collected from the flowers she grew, one of which was Antirrhinum, or 'Snapdragons.' I loved the name and watching the bees pushing their way in to gather the pollen. I would press either side of the flower to make it open for me. Then I would take delight in putting my finger into the opened flower and say 'Look Granma, it's biting my finger!'

I went to the local school at Button Oak, the next little village, just a short walk down the road. How I loved that walk, for wild flowers bloomed beautifully in the grass verges and the yellowhammers, pretty little birds, sang sweetly as they flew from twig to twig in the hedge, as if accompanying me on my journey. The hedge was resplendent in dog roses and honeysuckle during the late summer months and the smell was lovely.

The village consisted of one shop, a coal merchant, a public house, a telephone kiosk and a bus stop, together with a few houses. Little do I remember of any lessons, but I do remember very well the pantomime we 'put on' for Christmas. It was 'Hiawatha' and I was in my element, for I loved stories. I cannot remember now what part I had in the play, but I do remember we all had to recite the different parts of the story in poem form.

What I do remember very well was upsetting Granma! I had to recite a poem about 'Shoes' (what that had to do with Hiawatha I have no idea). It was only short and I put everything into it. It was about the shoes we would like. 'Red and pink and blue shoes,' but I don't think she understood that I wasn't complaining about the shoes that she bought me. When the poem went on to say 'but, fat shoes, flat shoes, wipe them on the mat shoes, stump along like that shoes, that's the sort they'll buy!' O dear! I did get a real telling off! She could not see that I did not mean it in a personal way.

I made friends with one little girl, but only during school time, for Granma liked to take me with her when she went to gather wood for the fire or while she was doing some other things. So, most of what play time I had, I rode a bicycle round and round the green, grassy area alone.

When I was about eight years old I had to change my school and go by bus to a school in Kinlet, another village further on into the country. I could not have been a pupil there for too long, as I have little memory of my time there.

Colds and sore throats were still a problem and so it was about this time that I found myself, with a few other children, in the children's ward at Kidderminster General Hospital for the removal of our tonsils and adenoids. We all looked like scared rabbits, not knowing what to expect, why we were there, or what was going to happen to us. In those days children were told nothing, and that, I think made it all the more frightening for us.

On the morrow we were taken to the operating theatre, one by one. I remember being wheeled down the corridor and seeing what looked like steps and wondering why the trolley didn't bump when we got to them. What I was seeing was the ceiling of course!

When I woke up, I had the worst sore throat that I had ever had! It seemed no time at all when we were being encouraged to drink cold water! It seemed so cruel at the time, but I know now just how important that is. Trying to eat corn flakes the next morning for breakfast seemed even worse, but I was allowed home and so I must have made a fair effort! I was so glad to go home the next day, but the soreness continued for some time.

When one of the neighbours heard that I had had the operation, she sent her daughter to the little shop in Button Oak and she brought me a small tub of ice cream with a little wooden spoon to eat it with. It was the loveliest thing I had ever tasted. What a shame my throat hurt so much! That was the very first time in my life that I had ever tasted ice cream!

Gradually the soreness subsided in my throat and I began to get a bit stronger in health and didn't get so many bad throats and bouts of ear pain.

When the cooler days came each year, the pig we had been fattening up to supply us with meat was slaughtered. How I hated that day! I would go into the house and put my fingers in my ears to drown out the pig's loud protests! What a busy time that was, for we had no fridges or freezers and all of the pig was prepared and eaten.

The 'flitches' (sides of bacon) were salted to cure them, as were the hams, and hung up in the living room over our heads until needed. Then they were let down on a rope and pulley, a few slices cut off, and then returned to their place again. The head and other bits were made into 'chawl', which was sliced like 'pressed meat', and the trotters were boiled and appeared on our plates.

'Faggots' were made from other internal bits of the pig. Even the intestines were washed, turned inside out on a stick to clean them and then cooked. They were called 'chitterlings' and these and the 'brains' were the only part I would not eat. What an array on the cold slab in the larder! We certainly ate well for a few days, but the rest of the year we lived on bacon and ham which was mostly fat, and the odd rabbit or occasional deer.

🔳 A move with a motive

There was a wooden bungalow next to our property, into which two single ladies came to live. One Sunday Dad was picking cherries from the tree adjacent to our property when these two ladies came past. They were smartly dressed in their Sunday best clothes complete with hats and gloves and carrying their Bibles. Granma was first to speak:

'Been to church then?'

'Yes,' they said, and smiled.

'Feel any better for it?'

They smiled again and went to move on, but just then a handful of cherries deftly landed at their feet, quickly followed by another. They looked up and were surprised to see a man smiling down at them and obviously much more amenable than his mother was. We became good friends and I enjoyed staying overnight in their 'guest room' in the bungalow. What a treat for a young child! It made me feel so grown up and very special. They took me on trips to various places and I grew to love them both.

As an 8 or 9 year old child, I didn't have any idea what was going on. Neither did the penny drop when we moved into a lovely old smallholding with four bedrooms called Gyn House. It had an elevated position with the most wonderful view I have ever seen, overlooking the River Severn as it flowed under the Victoria Bridge over which the steam trains travelled on their way between Bridgnorth and Kidderminster.

Arley village could be glimpsed between the trees and undulating landscape. The school, the church and the castle (before it was demolished) were also part of the lovely scene. Tiny farmsteads and cottages peeped out from among the trees on the wooded hillside opposite that was Eymore Wood and which rose up steeply on the other side of the river. Gyn House could not have been better situated.

How I loved that place! It was, I believe, a 400-year-old coaching inn made from honey coloured stone with a thick, heavy front door painted green with black studs, framed with beautiful yellow winter flowering jasmine. It was set in seven acres of land, comprising two fields set to pasture, an orchard in which grew many old varieties of apples, pears, damsons, cherries and plums, while in a large garden grew soft fruit and rhubarb, leaving ample space for potatoes and vegetables to supply a family for a whole year. A small flower garden ran from the back of the well and down the side of the property

Gyn House, Arley

where Dad had planted beautiful Hiawatha roses—they were a picture during the summer months.

There were four bedrooms, a large lounge with a huge inglenook fireplace and a large bay window. We lived in another large room because there was a big range to heat the room and do the cooking. The kettle could sing over the fire and bread could be toasted on a toasting fork before the red-hot embers behind the bars. Vegetables boiled in a saucepan over the hob and any meat sizzled as it cooked in the oven.

A big wooden screen with a seat served various purposes. It provided a seat for eating one's meal at the table, it cut the draught that seemed to whistle from under the door behind it and it housed the coats we used for the outside work as well as keeping them warm to put on when needed.

Three steps led up into the scullery, in which a brown sink with no outlet for water, and no water laid on, sprawled under a window. A baking oven and a copper for heating water for bathing and washing laundry filled the other side of the kitchen. Both had a place underneath for a fire to be lit to heat the water and bake the bread. The water came from the well on the yard just outside the back door. The water was so cold and refreshing and never ran dry. The well was, I believe, deeper than Bewdley Church! The well bucket held two ordinary pails of water and so was heavy to wind up when full. As this was the only means of water for the property, a lot of buckets of water had to be wound up from the depths, especially on wash day or bath day!

Even though it was older than the property we had just left, it was not so draughty. I was grateful for that because we still needed to use oil lamps and candles, as we had no electricity. Thankfully the candles were not in danger of being blown out.

The property was surrounded on three sides by Wyre Forest and the fourth side by a field, down which I would run to go to school in Arley village, having to cross over the River Severn by ferry. In summer when the river was low we had to cross by punt, rather dangerous when we were still only small children, but we knew the dangers and didn't misbehave! Otherwise the larger ferry was used and was connected to a strong wire. Perhaps it was to stop the ferry from being carried downstream when the current became very strong.

Two wonderful ferrymen took excellent care of us. In winter, when it was cold, I was allowed to go down into the cabin where it was lovely and warm, but when the river was in flood we couldn't go to school at all as the ferry could not run. I loved that because I was not fond of school. I had a problem with numbers and found it so embarrassing to always be bottom of the class. Mathematics was my worst subject. No one seemed to pick up on this or give me any help.

We increased our flock of chickens, sold the eggs, which had to be washed and graded, then packed ready for market. I enjoyed helping with this. We needed the extra money as the smallholding went with Dad's job, and so money was tight again. We also bought some cockerel chicks and fattened them up for the Christmas market.

I will never forget Granma and me sitting in the living room, the only place with a fire to keep us warm, plucking the feathers off these dead birds and getting them ready for market. We had feathers everywhere, floating about in the air, all over us, up our noses, in our hair, all over the furnishings—what a mess!

We didn't do that again! We didn't waste the feathers, though, as they were baked in the oven in small quantities to kill off any mites and seal the end of the quill, and then the old feathers from Granma's feather bed were thrown away and the new ones replaced them. We ate, breathed and dreamed feathers for weeks! However, a feather bed was wonderful to sleep on: so soft, warm and comfortable. It was well worth all the effort, but we never reared chickens for the Christmas market again!

I was given two lovely little bantam hens as pets. How proud I was of them! The one would fly to me when I called her and land on my shoulder. It was lovely to eat the little eggs for my breakfast.

Summers were very pleasant, not too hot—the temperature more constant with warm leisurely days and showers of rain from time to time. Occasionally there would be a thunderstorm. The meadows were lovely and green and filled with many summer flowers, as were the hedgerows. Birds were plentiful—singing their little hearts out the whole day long. We waited eagerly for the return of the migrating birds, like swifts and swallows, and the cuckoo was always heard.

How we loved to hear them! However, they were not so welcome when the fruit on the trees was ready for picking. They could strip the tree clean within minutes. We devised bird 'scarers' from pieces of sheet iron put into the trees against which we would bang an assortment of old bits of iron to make a noise to scare the little offenders away. The birds got up early though and one had to be up by 3 am if the fruit was to be saved for market! Why did I beg to be the one who got up to take the first shift? I was not alone, though, as a few of the neighbours were doing the same thing. The poor birds must have got very weary flying from one orchard to another, hardly managing to get one beak full of the delicious fruit before the noise drove them onto the next orchard.

Winters were not so welcomed by me. In fact, I dreaded them because I was always so cold and I shivered from the time I got up until I went to bed again. Fingers and toes were white and so painful, and it was agony when the blood started to flow in them again. Chilblains came on several of them, making them very uncomfortable. Even when sat by the fire, one's face burned but one's back froze. I was unaware then that I was troubled by Raynaud's disease. The frost made lovely patterns of leaves and ferns on the windowpanes overnight and any water left indoors in a container would be frozen by morning.

Leaving the warmth of the fire to go to bed in an icy bedroom was not something that I relished. I did have a warm nightdress and could keep my vest on and I had lovely woollen bed socks, but what about my head?

Granma had the answer. She cut the thick tops from her old lisle stockings and, sewing the two tops together, made a pixie style hat to keep my head and ears warm. Oh dear! Another dreaded pixie hat! What a sight I must have looked! At least, I was lovely and warm all night long!

Snow would start falling in November and last through to the end of March, or even longer. It was common to have four or five feet of snowfall overnight, which could then drift to many feet by morning, and if this happened to be against the outer door of the house, one had to dig oneself out before getting on with the work of the day. How I hated winters—they seemed to last far longer than in reality.

There was, however, one bright spot in winter and that was Christmas. I never expected any Christmas presents—we could not afford them anyway. However, I always had a book, 'The Girls' Annual' which I would read and reread through the year until I knew it by heart. It was also the one night in the year when I would go to bed without begging to stay up longer!

Our first Christmas at Gyn House was special. I had gone to bed without a murmur and was wakened by Dad coming to take me downstairs. I had no idea why. He carried his drowsy child to the living room door, which was closed. Then, blowing out the candle, he opened the door and my eyes widened in wonder and astonishment! The most enormous Christmas tree filled the corner of the room, beautifully decorated with pretty ornaments and real tiny candles which lit up the whole room. It was magical—I stared at it for a long time. I will always treasure the wonder of that moment.

What a difference it was in summer time, though. I would spend many hours playing alone in Wyre Forest. I knew where the foxes' dens were, where the badgers' setts were and where the squirrels' dreys were. Birds were recognised by their song and by their plumage. Trees were old friends, many of which I would climb and often hug. One tree was a particular favourite of mine—it was a beech tree with thirty-two trunks and I never failed to enjoy climbing among those and reading all the initials carved into its bark.

One thing I did avoid was the huge nests of forest ants. I did like to watch them going so energetically about their work, but moved quite smartly when one sunk his jaws into my toe. Wherever I went, I never felt lonely, fearful or in danger.

Working in Wyre Forest, Dad had opportunity from time to time to discover the chrysalises of moths and would bring them home in a matchbox. Each evening we would gently open the box, looking for signs of the moth emerging. I found it so exciting to watch as the moth tried to escape from the shell that had been its home while it developed into the beautiful creature that nature intended. Gently we would carry it back to where Dad had found it, and release it, after marvelling at the intricate patterns and colours in its delicate wings.

On moonlit nights, when the sky looked like deep blue velvet bejewelled with twinkling stars, Dad would take me into the forest to watch the fox cubs playing together, jumping over one another, Mum Fox watching over the youngsters while Dad Fox went off in search of food for his family. Sometimes we would visit a badger sett, watching patiently and silently until they cautiously emerged in the twilight. The young ones would play while the others searched for worms or beetles, cleaned out the sett (the place where they lived underground) and searched for new clean bedding, taking it into their home to make it clean and comfortable for them all. Sometimes playful fights occurred between them and it was hard not to laugh out loud at their antics. If we had made a noise they would have disappeared underground and our watching would be over for that evening.

Deer, too, came into the fields, jumping over the fence in search of juicy grass and remnants of hay, their eyes gleaming in the dark. If they sensed us there, two quick stamps of the front feet and they were off in a flash, leaping over the fence in an effort to guard their freedom.

What a delightful place Gyn House was! How I loved living there. Things, however, were afoot that I was not aware of that would change my life forever. I was to have a new mother. It was Beattie, one of the two ladies who lived in the bungalow next to us when we lived on Pound Green, and Dolly was coming, too, to be the sister Dad had 'always wanted but had never had'.

They had moved there from Smethwick, which I like to think of as the outskirts of Birmingham. They had both come from difficult home situations. Beattie had been turned out each night by a grandmother with whom she had gone to live after her parents had both died suddenly. The grandmother liked to have a drink of beer each evening and then, thinking Beattie an intruder, turned her out, leaving her to walk the streets each night.

Dolly was from a home where she was abused, going to work only to have to hand over her wages each week to her father, and she was beaten by her siblings. She also cared for her sick mother and did all the housework and washing. They both saw the advertisements about the opening of a place of worship called Hebron Hall. This new gospel hall was a place to be warm, have a cup of hot tea and a bite to eat. That is where they met, and when they learned of each other's circumstances they decided to rent a room together and be free of their situations. However, they had to wait until Dolly was twenty one years of age as she could not, by law, leave home until that time, and that is what they did.

I was delighted that Beattie would be my new mother, as now I would be like other children. Perhaps I would have not been so delighted if I had known that my behaviour was causing a great deal of concern. I had become very disobedient to Granma, refusing to obey when she asked me to do something like make the fire up to stop it going out, or peel the potatoes for the evening meal. I would stamp my foot and say 'I won't'—not to her face but behind her back. I thought she didn't see me, but I found that she did have eyes in the back of her head as she said!

I had discovered books. Not that we could afford to buy books, but I could borrow them from the travelling library that visited the school each week. They were so exciting that with my nose in a book I lost all sense of time. It was no good—something had to be done! I needed a firmer hand before I became totally out of control!

Hard lessons to learn

It was a very excited 11-year-old child, sitting in a beribboned, highly polished car, dressed in a long, beautiful, turquoise blue velvet dress with tulip sleeves, a circle of spring flowers adorning her head, matching the posy of flowers she carried in her hands. Dolly, similarly dressed, accompanied her as they made their way from Pound Green to the church in Arley village for the wedding of Dad and Beattie, my new Mum.

Nothing so wonderful had ever happened to me before, and my excitement knew no bounds. After the ceremony and the taking of

Dad marrying Beatrice (known as Beattie)
and Eunice and Dolly as bridesmaids

photos had been completed, we made our way back to my new Auntie's house where the wedding reception was being held. I was surprised to find that new members were now added to the family.

Later that night, and back at home, I was still very much on a high.

Missing Dolly, who had come into the family, as Dad said, 'to be the sister he never had', I went looking for her. I ran up the stairs and found her bedroom door closed, and without thinking I burst in and stopped dead.

'What are you doing I asked?'

She was kneeling on the floor at the foot of her bed. She smiled, held out her hand to me and said, 'Come.'

I shut the door behind me and joined her on the floor. 'What are you doing?' I repeated.

'I'm praying and reading my Bible' she said. 'I am a Christian and I love the Lord Jesus.'

She picked up her Bible and opened it up to the Gospel of John and she turned to Chapter 3 and started to read from verse 16. These are the words she read: 'For God so loved the world that He gave His only begotten Son that whoever believes in Him shall not perish but have eternal life. For God did not send His Son into the world to condemn the world but to save the world through Him. Whoever believes in Him is not condemned, but whoever does not believe stands condemned already because He has not believed in the name of God's only begotten Son.'

She told me to put my name in there; so this is what I read: 'For God so loved Eunice that He gave His only begotten Son, that if she believes in Him she should not perish but have eternal life.'

I did not need to read any more because I saw it so clearly. I saw that my behaviour of late was very naughty and deserved punishment. I got up and, as I did, I saw in the mirror behind me a small cross and a figure hung on it. I realised that God was showing me my Saviour on a cross dying for me. I went to my room next door and got out a small Bible which had been given to me by my Granma a short time before. I got onto my knees by the side of my bed and prayed, 'Father God, I am sorry for my naughty ways. Please forgive me and save me from my sin. Thank you for sending your Son to die in my place for my sin. Please make me clean and help me to be good. Lord Jesus, thank you for dying for me on the cross. Please come into my heart and be my saviour. Help me to live to please you. Thank you. Amen.'

I felt a joy sweep through me and a feeling of peace and I knew He had heard and answered my prayer. How I was going to need Him through the days ahead, and how thankful I was that He knew that and had come to me ready to help me through each day. As I could see such a change in my behaviour, I thought the family would know I had become a Christian and I didn't think I needed to tell them. It was years later before I did. I tried hard to please and life was wonderful in many ways.

I was taken to a new relative who had a clothing shop and was bought some new clothes. I couldn't believe it. I was kitted out from head to foot, from underclothes to a mauve coat and hat, gloves and shoes. It was a proud little girl who went back to school after the summer break in a new outfit.

I had never seen my Dad so happy. I was thrilled for him. Poor Granma seemed far from happy, though. However, it soon became evident that Dad had been told, 'Leave the correcting of your daughter to me.' It didn't take me long to realise this and I saw the pain in his eyes each time I misbehaved and needed to be corrected. The trouble was, I often didn't know what I had done wrong! As I have grown older I have been able to understand a little of what poor Beattie must have been going through and why she acted as she did.

It was about this time that my sister Beryl met the man of her dreams, Reg, and they began planning their wedding. The ceremony was to be at Arley Church and I was to be a bridesmaid and Reg's sister, Iris, also. What excitement again! Dad agreed to their wedding and to give her away and the reception was to be at Gyn House. This time they were to cross the river and walk the short distance up to the Church from the ferry.

My sister, by this time, had changed her place of work and worked in Kidderminster. Her employers had gone on holiday and Beryl was living in the property. They asked if they could have their honeymoon there until they returned and then go into the house, which Beryl had been preparing while Reg was in the Army in Germany. Reg's brother Cyril was his best man.

How special Iris and I felt crossing over the river dressed in our beautiful pink dresses! After the wedding, photos were taken and then it was up the short drive to Gyn House and a rather longer walk up the field with the cows wondering at this strange sight.

What a spread met our eyes as we entered the big front room and saw the tables laid out with the wedding breakfast! The lovely day

Beryl and Reg's wedding (Eunice as bridesmaid)

seemed to be all too quickly over for me, However, the animals needed to eat and drink too, so they had to be thought of as well.

For Reg it was 'Army days' and Beryl preparing the home they would share together until her death after a long and happy marriage. They were blessed with two beautiful daughters. The eldest, Susan, lost her battle with cancer a few years ago, but thankfully, Melonie is doing a great job caring for her Dad in spite of her own health problems and working.

We bought a cow called Janey, and her calf, who gave us all the milk we needed as well as butter and cream. A pig was being fattened up for market, which also benefited from the leftover milk. We also had three bullocks, perhaps to keep the grass down in the fields, and to sell when they were ready for market, for we were always desperate for money.

I tried to be helpful and had one day gone to meet Beattie arriving on the bus from town, where she had gone to pay for the animals' food and buy the groceries for the week. I thought I could help to carry the groceries home. When she realised why I had come, she burst into tears. After paying for

Cows at Gyn House

Pigs at Gyn House

the animals' food, she only had enough money to buy a swede! We carried it home between us, each holding a handle of the bag.

Wanting to be more helpful, I started to do other jobs around home. I saw the forest was starting to grow through into the fields, so asked if I could take a small bill hook and cut back the intruding growth to keep the fields clear.

There were several old tree stumps that needed to be removed from the orchard, so I enjoyed removing these. Each week the chicken house needed cleaning out, so I took that as my job too. The hardest job, though, was to water the cattle morning and evening, drawing the water up from the well and carrying the two buckets of water up the orchard and into the field where the cattle were, and filling the metal bath to the top.

I filled it before I went to school and again when I came home from school. The cattle would be waiting for it and drink from the buckets before I could tip them into the bath. In summer the bath would be empty both before I went to school and again when I returned. However, in winter the water in the bath would be frozen and I had to remove the ice before I could fill the container up. Not easy when thirsty animals were jostling each other to get a drink. It was dangerous for a small, weak child to be in such a situation, but thankfully I was kept from harm. I believe that God had his hand over my life and took care of me on many occasions.

On one winter morning, snow had fallen and it had been freezing hard for some days and the ground was very icy and dangerous to walk on. The cattle still needed to drink and I went out dressed for the weather to draw the water up from the well for them. The well had a wooden covering and a board at the front which was hinged, so it could be folded down to enable the bucket, when wound up full of water, to be caught and lifted on to the yard. You may remember my saying that the well bucket held two standard pails of water.

There was a flat board in front of the well, to stand on as one leaned over the well to take hold of the bucket as it reached the top. I was very used to winding up the water, but on this occasion it was very near to a disaster. I wound the bucket up all right and then went to lift it onto the yard when my foot slipped on the icy board and I fell over the half board and hovered half over the well. Fortunately I had let go of the well bucket which tore back down the well again at an alarming rate. My screams brought the family running to my aid. Someone else watered the cattle for me as I trembled with the shock of what had happened.

I didn't go to school that day, and it was just the day that the attendance officer came to the school to check up on any absentees. He came to the house to see why I was absent, but when he heard what had happened and how I was shaking and crying at the awful memory of what could have happened, he understood and went away satisfied that I was not playing truant!

Next morning I was back on the job again, singing my heart out as usual, but I made sure that the ice was cleared away from the well area before I started winding the water up from the well! It was a lesson well learned.

I stopped having the books from the travelling library that visited the school each week, as I found wonderfully exciting stories in my Bible that I read under the bed covers by torchlight each night. Stories of battles, miracles, dreams where God spoke to people, fingers writing a message on the wall, and lots more—and they were true!

How I loved the 'everyday' things in nature that were happening around me. I seemed to see them with fresh eyes now I was a Christian. The beautiful wild flowers growing in the hedgerows, the glorious patches of bluebells in the forest, the grass with the wild flowers in the meadow, that Dad would cut with a scythe to make sweet-smelling hay for feeding the cattle during the winter months.

We would turn it several times until it was ready to be gathered to make into a hayrick, then we piled the hay onto the rick sheet to drag it down the field to Dad. We then pitched it up to him with our pitchforks and then returned for another load while he placed the new hay carefully, making sure that the rain would not penetrate and spoil that for which we had laboured so hard, until all was gathered in safely. It was then used, as needed, to feed the cattle during the long winter months when the grass was not growing and the white blanket of snow covered everything.

I loved looking up into the beautiful starry sky at night, for it was a wonderful sight with no light pollution to spoil it. I was amazed at the greatness of our God, who had created such a beautiful world for us to live in: the birds always singing their hearts out as they helped themselves to the bounty their heavenly Father had provided; the little baby chicks that hatched from the eggs the mother hen had so beautifully and faithfully tended, turning the eggs carefully, keeping them warm with her downy feathers, then searching for food and calling them to come and taste with her encouraging clucks after they had successfully hatched; then her urgent, anxious calls as danger posed a threat to her dear little family. They didn't wander far from mom, and ran quickly to her when they heard her calling, popping quickly under her wings and nestling close to her warm body. What a lovely picture that was to me of God's care, provision and protection of us. I would try to picture what it was like for those little chickens being warm and cosy and safe from predators and hearing their mother's heartbeat as they nestled so close to her.

Sometimes when I went to bed in tears, after yet again not behaving as I should have done, I would read from the Gospel of Matthew, chapter 23 and verse 37 where the Lord Jesus said 'O Jerusalem, Jerusalem, how oft would I have gathered you under my wings as a hen gathers her chicks, but you would not.' I would try to imagine what it would be like to be warm and comfy, safe under His wings, hearing His very heartbeat, knowing that He understood and felt the pain with me. Somehow I just knew that He did and it comforted me.

What a blessing Dolly was to me at that time. She wisely guided me in my understanding of each difficult situation I found myself in, and tried to show me better ways. Never did she take sides but helped me to see my own errors. We would go for walks together in the forest and sing choruses and she would help me to see where I was making mistakes. God had known that I would need her also, and not only gave me a new mother but a new wonderful friend as well.

I felt I was improving, but there was one problem that I did not seem able to overcome. I had a dreadful temper, and when I lost my temper I would scream, shout and totally lose it. It had to be dealt with, and quickly.

Again, we needed money and were fattening up the pig for market—it was almost at the right weight when it objected to my two pet bantam chickens sharing its dinner. I saw red when I noticed some feathers and part of a wing in the pig's sty. I screamed, shouted, stamped my feet and told the pig, 'You ought to die!' I then caught Dad looking at me. The pain on his face stopped me and I ran to my room sobbing.

The mood was still very sombre the next morning when I came to the breakfast table. Dad came in from feeding the animals, sat down heavily and said, 'Pig's dead'. I froze! 'I've killed the pig,' I thought. I put a curse on it and killed it and now there is no pig, no money and a vet's bill to pay. I was horrified.

I was not in the habit of apologising, but I did then. It was not I, though, that had killed the pig. It was the pig's own fault. The chicken bones it had eaten had splintered and pierced the pig's gut. That was what had killed it, not any special powers from me. It taught me a lesson that I needed to learn. From that day to this, I have never lost my temper like that again. Kindly, no one said anything. They saw that I had learnt an important lesson and were silent.

Defying Dad

The time came for me to take my 11-plus exam. As we were always so short of money, I reasoned that I could not possibly be successful. It would not be right for Dad to have to make the decision not to send me to High School if I passed. Money for uniform, books, train fares and fees would be needed—no, I must not pass and put him in that situation. So I sent in a nearly blank exam paper. When the results came in and they saw I had failed, they didn't turn a hair. I think they expected it somehow.

One day I found a tiny book with Beattie's name in it, and I asked her about it. It was a St John Ambulance book on First Aid. I was amazed to hear that she had wanted to go to Nigeria as a missionary. I was full of questions and I discovered that she had passed all the exams but had failed on health grounds. I was eager to know more. She pointed to her neck and said that because her neck was 'full', the doctors had said that she would have died after a few weeks, as she had a problem with a goitre. She didn't believe them and still wanted to go, but the door had closed and there was nothing she could do about it. I felt so sorry for her, as I know how she would have felt. In later years, the doctors were proved right and she needed surgery on her thyroid gland.

So the days went by and my time for leaving school was drawing nearer and I decided to consider my options. These didn't seem to be many. I hated housework and could not conceive of myself spending the rest of my life doing that. I could work in a garden centre, but as my maths was not good I could not be on the till giving change to people. To sow seeds and prick out seedlings was not an option either, as I felt the cold so badly and would have been unable to handle tiny seedlings with numb fingers. Working in a factory was definitely out as Dad absolutely forbade that. What was I to do?

There was one thing that I loved to do—when anyone was sick I would beg to stay home and care for them and nurse them. Of course, I was never allowed to, no matter how hard I pleaded. I had to wait until the weekend came to care for them. A seed, though, had been planted in my heart and was growing well. The more I considered it, the better it sounded and the more I liked it. Was it planted by God? I liked to think it was.

So, the time came for us to decide our futures and we had to see the Job Opportunities Officer at the school together with our parents. Beattie and Dad were expecting me to go into service, the dreaded housework job. They were shocked when I said, 'I want to be a nurse.' They stared at me, eyes wide, mouths open, as if they hadn't heard right. The Officer looked from them to me and back to them again. They tried all ways to make me change my mind, but it was made up. 'It will be long hours, it will be poor pay—you will see dreadful sights, there will be blood and other nasty things to deal with.' But no matter what they said, my mind was made up and nothing was going to change it.

Never before had I ever refused to obey my Dad. I did not understand why I felt as strongly as I did. I somehow knew that was what I had to do. It wasn't until I said, 'Well, Dad, it's nursing or nothing,' that he said, 'Well, you had better go and be a nurse then, because I can't keep you for the rest of your life.' I was delighted. Now I would work hard and I would be the best nurse I could possibly be.

Then a bombshell! I discovered that I would have to stay on at school for another year! Knowing how I hated school, Dad thought I would change my mind. But I didn't turn a hair, even being willing to go to Stourport Secondary Modern School to study anatomy, physiology and hygiene with two other girls on our own for twelve months. This meant that I had to catch the 7 am train from Arley station to Stourport. I would run down the field and join the road at the bottom, meeting another friend who was also running to catch the train, and we would run together to catch the transport (the Severn Valley Railway now) going on to our different destinations.

There was, however, a problem! This train got me into Stourport with quite a wait on my hands before school started. So it was arranged that a very kind lady in Stourport open her home to me each school morning. She greeted me with a blazing fire to warm me up on cold mornings and a mug of hot tea and hot buttered toast, saying to me, 'When you are ready to go, just drop the catch,' and she went off to work. I've never forgotten the kindness of that dear lady. I believe she was one of God's angels.

The year went by quickly and I then joined others and we became nursing cadets at Mill Street General Hospital, working in the different departments, helping where we could for two years. I worked in the outpatients department, pharmacy, physiotherapy, theatre and children's ward. This gave us an introduction into each department and an understanding as to what they did and how they functioned. I loved every minute of it. Two days in the week we went to college in Bromsgrove to study anatomy, physiology and hygiene.

At home, however, things were not as well as they might have been. Beattie was worried about Dad's health. He went to the doctor at her request, only to be told, 'There is nothing wrong that the summer will not put right.' She was not satisfied and asked him to get a second opinion. The news was not good. He was suffering from the disease that his first wife had died from, pulmonary tuberculosis. He could not work and had to go to bed and stay there, taking drugs that were not available to my mother when she was so ill.

However, he grew worse and I found myself about 2 am one morning running to my Auntie's house to ask her to phone for the doctor to attend. Dad was transferred to Knightwick Hospital the next day where they treated people with pulmonary tuberculosis. We were stunned and very upset that the first doctor could have got it so wrong. We were talking about taking it further but Dad asked us not to. 'Please forgive him, we can all make mistakes,' he said. 'Don't take the bread out of his children's mouths.' How this showed his kind, gentle nature!

Still the animals needed to be cared for. Janey the cow needed to be milked twice a day and so we were dependent on my Auntie's family and neighbours. Everyone was so helpful and we were so glad of all the help given. Now Dad's wage was reduced to sick pay, but I was able to add the tiny bit I had left after paying my bus fares to get to work at the hospital. They were hard days fraught with uncertainty, but none of us ever doubted that things would get better. Dad would come home healed and things would be fine. He began to put on weight and to look much healthier. How we looked forward to the report brought to us after each visit by Beattie and whichever one of us went with her to visit him each week.

As the months went by, Dad began to get weary of waiting for the healing process to be complete and asked the consultant about surgery. He said he could operate, but was very reluctant to do so because of his age. However, Dad kept asking for surgery, until he gave way and reluctantly agreed to perform the surgery required. He was transferred to a hospital in Malvern and the surgery took place. He had one lung removed and also one third of the other. His life hung in the balance for days. He reacted badly to the needed medication, having to suffer the pain that the offending drugs would have relieved. He was a battler though, and slowly but surely he began to win through. News was good, and soon there was talk of his coming home. We were thrilled and looked forward to that day.

Chapter 4

On visiting Dad one day, Beattie thought he looked pale and mentioned this to the sister on the ward before she left to get the transport home. On her arrival at home she found her nephew waiting to urgently take her back to the hospital. They were, however, too late. He died before they got there. The postmortem showed that a duodenal ulcer had eroded an artery and death had come quickly and painlessly.

We were devastated. Poor Beattie was beside herself. It was March and snow covered the ground. It was so cold. My only memory is of going into town to buy black clothes for the funeral and then walking down the hill from the church after the funeral. All other painful memories have mercifully been erased except one.

After arriving home from the funeral, my aunts on my mother's side came back to the house and said, 'You won't want her anymore,' pointing to me. 'We'll take her.'

I was horrified; I did not really know them. I'd had very little to do with my mother's side of the family and had never met some of my cousins. I didn't even know their names. What about Granma? I had never known life without her. She had been a mother as well as grandmother to me. How could I go and leave her? My world was tumbling around me. How could this be happening? Leave my new mother at such a difficult time as this? Leave Dolly, my mentor, friend and spiritual mother? What would Beattie say? I turned to look at her. It seemed an age before she said,

'I think we should let her decide for herself,' then, turning her tear-stained face to me she said, 'Do you want to go?'

'No, I want to stay with you.'

She turned to my dry-eyed aunties and said, 'That's how it will be, then, she stays with us.'

They got up to leave and I went to Beattie and hugged her. 'Thank you, thank you,' I said, so relieved that we could stay together.

Within two weeks we had notice to vacate our beloved Gyn House! Somehow the animals were sold, the chickens went to market, the two dogs put to sleep as were the seven cats, all except two that is, for they escaped and we never found them. We had to leave too, but where were we to go? None of us could think straight. We contacted the local counsellor and he told us of a vacant property on the other side of the river, into which we gratefully moved. Although it was a nice house, not one of us felt that we could settle and I had reason more than any of the others to be very uncomfortable in that house.

All of us were hit very hard by Dad's death, but Beattie was really struggling and we began to fear that she would not survive. As she had not been married quite five years, she could not claim widow's pension and was forced to look for a job. She became a home help, but in the rural community had to walk between clients, reducing the number of clients she could help each day and thus reducing what she could earn. The bus service didn't coincide with her work needs.

Dolly continued with her work in the factory, Granma sitting in her chair reminiscing, and I with my work as a cadet nurse at the local hospital and continuing the two days each week at the College of Further Education in Bromsgrove. I would soon be 17 and able, after another year, to start my nursing training to become a State Registered Nurse.

I was very angry at God and told Him, 'I don't want You in my life anymore, if that is what you do to me, taking my beloved Dad as well as my Mom. That's it, I will go my own way.' It was a dangerous time in my life as Rock 'n Roll had become fashionable. The music of the day replaced lovely hymns and choruses that I had sung with such delight and relish. My Bible lay unopened. This added to the pain that was so keenly felt by the others too, I'm sure.

A problem shared was a problem understood

Let me go back to the house we had moved into. Even though it was a lovely property and very adequate for our needs, I hated it. It was not that I longed for Gyn House and all the animals. In a way I did, but this was not the reason at all. It was the bedroom I was in. At first all was well, but as time went on something began to happen. I would wake up and become aware of bells ringing very faintly and then fade away. A short time later it would happen again, only a bit louder. Each time, it was getting slightly louder and then it began happening more than once each night.

I began dreading going to bed, as I had begun to feel as if the pressure of hands were around my neck, gently at first, but increasing each time, until I was finding it difficult to breathe. I didn't say anything to anyone about what was going on as I thought they would think I was reacting badly to losing Dad or becoming mentally ill. I didn't want to worry them. It got to the stage where I began dreading going home, but I couldn't stop as they would have wanted to know why. I was terrified to go to bed and I felt I was in a helpless situation, one I could do nothing about. All the time, the bells were getting louder and the hands round my throat were getting tighter, and it was happening several times each night. I was getting more and more terrified and quite unable to sleep.

One day Beattie said, out of the blue, 'Why don't we buy a house in Kidderminster?' I could hardly believe my ears. I was all for it and heartily endorsed it. Oh joy, I would soon be out of this house, I thought, and away from the situation in that bedroom. But what I didn't realise was that the property was yet to be built!

My cadet days were ending and I sat my exams to enter training to be a State Registered Nurse. English and Maths were part of the exam—what else I cannot now remember. Amazingly I passed. How I had managed to pass the Maths part I will never know, but I had. The first three months we spent in Bromsgrove General Hospital, joining together with students from there, for the Preliminary Training School. It was an intensive three-month training studying anatomy, physiology, hygiene and nursing, together with other subjects that have escaped my memory.

For the first year of my three-year training, I had to live in at the hospital, going home on my days off. However, I still dreaded going home—not that I didn't want to see my family but because of what happened each night. I was so looking forward to our new property in Kidderminster, but it seemed to be taking ages. Dolly would go most work days and bring back a report of how much had been completed. I discovered, though, that when you wait for something so eagerly the waiting could seem endless.

As most of us who were about to start our nurses' training were only 18, the hospital was responsible for us until we came of age at 21 years. It was a strange new alien world that I had moved into as I walked through the door to the nurses' home, feeling quite grown up. All my life, I had lived with older people and it seemed so strange to be with people my own age. There were rules to be observed, as one had to be in the nurses' home by 9.30pm and in bed by 10pm with lights out. The night sister came round each night to check, and if your bed was empty you found yourself in Matron's office the next morning, giving an explanation for your absence. Your excuse had to be a good one!

Our new uniforms were on our beds ready to be worn on the ward the next day. We would only find out which ward on the morrow! Blue and white striped dresses, white highly starched bibbed aprons, neat little white starched caps (although I think that for the first year we wore butterfly caps, but I can't be quite sure) and a blue and white striped belt, as well as the black shoes and stockings which we had to provide ourselves. These completed our uniforms. As I looked at that uniform on the bed, I thought, 'Tomorrow I will really start my journey to train to be a nurse—a real one,' and a thrill of excitement ran through me tinged with apprehension.

How nervous we felt as we presented for duty next morning! I think I was sent to Female Medical—it was a small ward for which I was thankful, as I was taken round the patients by the senior staff nurse who told me to get a pen and paper to write down the names of the patients and their diagnoses. How out of place and stupid we felt when we fell for the tricks played on most of the new recruits. We soon settled down, though, and became useful members of the team, helping those dear sick people get better again. I felt in my element. I loved it so much that I didn't want to go off-duty. I soon learnt that I needed to care for myself if I was to be of any use in caring for others.

I grew to love every stone of that hospital. It was not big by today's standards—just 100 beds, but it was adequate for the needs of the day. However, we could always find a place to put up an extra bed if we needed to. Male and female medical wards, male and female surgical wards, a children's ward, male and female accident unit, a casualty department, a diagnostic laboratory, physiotherapy department, an X-ray department, a laundry and, most importantly, a large kitchen where all the meals were cooked for patients and staff alike.

My favourite part was the main hall where the main staircase swept down from the second floor to the ground floor, turning on itself half way down. Behind it was the most beautiful stained glass window that cast beautiful coloured light as the sun poured through it onto the floor and furniture in the hall.

I was not working on the female medical ward for many weeks when I was moved onto the accident unit on day duty. The patients, who were mainly younger men, delighted playing tricks on the new, still wet-behind-the-ears nurse, who soon learned to give as good as she took!—although I found it very hard at first.

Late one afternoon, there were three of us on the ward of about twenty-five patients. The staff nurse in charge went on her tea break, leaving an extremely good male nursing auxiliary and me on the ward. Noticing a patient didn't look right, I shouted to the auxiliary to come as I ran towards the ill man. 'Press that bell' he shouted, and I ran to do it. Within seconds, doctors, the staff nurse who had been on her break, and it seemed to be so many more—even the hospital's porter—were fighting to save the life of the critically ill patient. This was my first encounter with death.

Shortly afterwards, I found myself on the female medical ward again, but this time on night duty. I went onto the ward and the nurse gave me the report and left. I was alone and scared! What did I have to do? I didn't have a clue! I went down the patients and with my trusty bit of paper that I had written down the names and diagnoses on, familiarised myself with the patients before the night sister came to do her round. When I got to the last patient, she didn't seem right and just then the door opened and the night sister walked in.

The poor lady was in hospital because her diabetes was unstable and she was just suffering an attack at that moment. I did not have a clue what to do but rushed to the kitchen to get some glucose in some milk at Sister's command. It was too late though, she could not drink it, and a doctor had to come to inject some glucose into her vein. When the doctor had gone and the patient was fine again, the night sister tore me off a strip, making me feel very guilty. She even shouted at me for running to get the milk. 'One only ran' she informed me, 'when someone was haemorrhaging or there was a fire'!

She could have died, I thought, and it would have been my fault. The poor lady didn't get too much sleep that night as I kept waking her up to make sure she was all right. The next night, it happened again, and the next. The problem was that she was going into a coma before I even got on to the ward. She was not my favourite patient just at that time and I was certainly not Night Sister's favourite nurse. Come to think of it, she was certainly not my favourite Night Sister either!

Christmas was a magical time at the hospital. Each ward chose a theme and we all worked on the decorations, staying on the ward to make decorations when our shift was ended. Each one wanted to be the best when our efforts were judged. How well I remember on Christmas Eve, all the nurses congregating in the main hall, each one in uniform with her navy blue cloak turned inside out showing the red interior. Each one carried a lantern on a short stick. The lights were extinguished and we started to sing carols as we walked very slowly down corridors and into each ward. Matron always walked with us. It was so effective and very moving and really appreciated by the patients.

While on night duty on the female surgical ward one night, I went to a lady who could not sleep. She wanted to talk and shared with me what had happened to her. That poor lady had gone through a dreadful time, and it seemed to help her to share it. In the course of our conversation, she mentioned where she had lived at that time. I was amazed to hear that it was exactly where we were living now. Now I understood why I was having the problem each night with the bells and the feeling of being choked!

Thinking straight again

We were watching with great excitement the finishing touches to our new home in Kidderminster, and at last it was ours. The keys were handed to us and we moved in with the snow on the ground in March. Beattie, Dolly, Granma, Peter the Budgie (who didn't survive unfortunately) and me. What excitement! It was cold and damp (the walls felt wet as the property dried out) and we shivered as we huddled around the tiny electric fire or the wood and coal fire, where the heat went up the chimney and not into the room!

However, I was free from that awful bedroom at last. How I rejoiced and revelled in a full night's sleep. No longer did I have to battle the two steep and winding hills on my bicycle to have it at home for the journey to work on Sunday mornings when there was no bus service running. Those two hills after a day's shift were nearly the end of me. Now they were behind me too. It was so exciting, arranging our new home and meeting the new neighbours who were moving in as we were. We were on the very edge of town and had quite a bit of countryside around us still, which we really appreciated. I was able to cycle to work after my first year of compulsory 'living in' as the hospital was only at the end of the road. Returning home at the end of my shift was a different story, especially when I was on night duty. I was so tired that I found myself falling asleep as I cycled, and if I walked, I found myself falling asleep as I took a step!

We began thinking about a church to go to and went to a service in various places of worship, but didn't feel at home in any of them.

Chapter 6

In the market in town, we discovered a Bible stall, and on talking to the person who was selling the literature found there were two places that we might find suitable. One was at Norton, Stourbridge and the other was in Areley Kings. Both were a distance away and we had no transport and buses didn't run on Sundays. Through the Bible stall we met others who did go to both and had transport. They were also willing to give us a lift from time to time. We felt at home at both places of worship.

We realised how needful a car was and I made up my mind to start a car fund. However, my wages were very poor. But bearing in mind that I was being trained as a State Registered Nurse and not having to pay any fees for this, I couldn't expect to get much in the way of wages! I made a decision to have only seven pounds (old money) each month for my use and to put the other into a 'Car Fund'. My family supported me by providing food, etc. Any left over at the end of the month also went into the fund. Gradually it started to grow, and when it was nearing a suitable amount I started to take driving lessons.

We began attending the church at Areley Kings more regularly now, as and when transport was available, but we, and the couple who usually provided the transport, Frank and Mary, felt that we needed a church in Kidderminster. Not long after we had started to attend church more regularly, two young men came from a Bible training school at Dawlish to hold a campaign at the church and we were thrilled to get involved as we were able.

While they were there, I began to think very seriously about my relationship with God. I thought more of what it would have been like if Dad had recovered and what life would have been like for him. He would never have been able to work again, and we would have had to leave Gyn House, sell all the livestock, get rid of the pets and he would have seen all this. Dad would have had to take part in it and be aware that it was because of his condition. It would have upset him so much.

What is more, he was also going blind 'with bleeding at the back of the eyes' as the eye consultant had said. For him, life would have been very difficult. I began to see how good God was in taking my dear Dad to Himself, and that is what happened, for I knew my Dad trusted the Lord for salvation as I did. He was a true Christian.

I came to God and thanked Him for being so kind to my Dad and saving him from the awful life he would have had if our prayers for him had been answered. I sought His forgiveness for my attitude towards Him, for not trusting Him to do his very best for us. I welcomed Him into my life again to be my Saviour and my Lord, to help me to trust Him, and rely on Him as I went through life. I gave myself to Him for whatever He wanted for my life. Little did I know the significance of my words to the Lord at that moment, but He took me at my word. He came into my life and began to work out His purposes from that time on.

It was so wonderful to be again connected to the God I had turned to so many times before as I had been hurting, while I was being knocked into shape. Again, His word, the Bible, became precious to me as I began to read it more and more. How it spoke to me in my situation, giving me guidance, teaching me, helping me to see things clearly where before I had not understood the meaning. Still I did not say anything to the family, feeling, I suppose, that these were private matters between God and me. How they would have rejoiced at my news! How the whole church would have rejoiced together!

One of the young men, on hearing that I was a nurse at the local hospital, asked if there was a Nurses' Christian Fellowship there. As a result, I found myself trembling outside the door of Matron's office as I gently tapped on the door to her office and waited for her 'Come in.' When I went in and asked her if I could have her permission to start a Nurses' Christian Fellowship, she asked all about it and what it would entail. She seemed satisfied and gave her permission.

Chapter 6

I closed the door behind me and then realised what I had done. I was now responsible for the weekly meeting for hospital staff. What had I committed myself to?

I was the shyest person possible and had never stood up before a group of people before. (The first time we met, I woke up with a rash from head to toe! It must have been nerves as it went as soon as the meeting was over!)

I was thinking, 'I will get the person I had invited to speak and they can do what is needed.' I found however, it didn't quite work out that way. Often I would be called on to say something or open in prayer and I would find it so difficult, but I was thrilled how people from the hospital came along, as well as friends to support me. God had a plan, though, that I was not aware of.

There were some young people at the church at Areley Kings, one of whom was Heather. We decided to go to a young people's house group together at Grange-over-Sands in Cumbria. As the time approached, we got quite excited at the thought of our holiday. However, on the morning that we were to go, we were woken up by Heather's frantic knocking on the door. We had all overslept! Never have I moved so fast in my life. In less than ten minutes we were in her dad's car racing to the pick-up point, but when we got there the coach had already left! I felt dreadful as I sat pleading with God to get us on the coach as Heather's father, hunched over the steering wheel, pushed the old car to its limits. Never had it gone so fast in its life before, and we spotted the coach before we reached the next pick-up point, where we were able to board it.

We had a really lovely holiday by the sea and found the time with other young folk refreshing. The day was ours to do as we pleased and the evenings were taken up with singing, testimonies and finished with a special speaker, most of whom were missionaries. We found it all so lovely and uplifting, but one evening was particularly wonderful for me. The speakers were an elderly couple, the Rev. and Mrs Herbert Jenkinson, who had worked as missionaries in what was then Belgian Congo. They were known as 'the Kinso's' and they told us of the work they had been doing among the people whose lives were lived in the fear of evil spirits.

Everything was controlled by witch doctors. It was to them that the people went if one was sick, or to make the garden produce a good crop, or to give success in hunting for food. One could also buy a curse to put on an enemy and they lived in fear all the time of someone putting a curse on them!

They told of how the witch doctors, dressed in animal skins, their bodies painted with dyes they gathered from the forest where they lived, and adorned with bird's feathers, leaves and animal bones, terrified the people. They were frightening to look at, invoking fear in the people and demanded high prices for their services, which often did not work. This for these dear people was life—a life of fear, worry and anxiety. The evil spirits had to be appeased, but one never knew if or how one had displeased them!

As they were talking, I thought of these poor people kept bound by these wicked, evil witch doctors for their gain and profit, with no concern at all for the folk held in fear and bondage by their greed.

There were no medical doctors or hospitals to help them if they were sick. My heart went out to these poor folk. How they needed help! We then sang a song to finish. It was:

Every person in every nation
in each succeeding generation
has the right to hear the news that Christ can save.

Crucified on Calvary's mountain,
He opened wide a crystal fountain,
Conquered sin, and death and hell
and rose up from the grave.
Master, I am willing to dedicate to thee,
life and talent, time and money; here am I, send me.

As I sang those words, I really did mean every one of them. As I thought of what God had done for me, sending His Son to die on the cross at Calvary to bear my sin. I thought of my life, all my naughty ways as a child, and even now as I had grown older. Thoughts that should never have been thought, things I would be ashamed for anyone else to know. I knew I was a sinner. God says we are 'born in sin and shaped in iniquity,' but I was saved by God's amazing grace, when I confessed my sin to Him and asked His forgiveness as I knelt beside my bed as an eleven-year-old child.

I realised that we don't stand a chance, for we are all born into this world with a sinful nature. It is normal to sin; we don't have to be taught to sin. Sinning comes naturally enough. For heaven to be a reality, that sin needs to be dealt with and only the blood of Jesus is sufficient for that. My mind went back to the day I had knelt by my bed and confessed my sinfulness to God, asked His forgiveness and cleansing in the precious blood of Jesus and then asked Him to come into my life and be my saviour. I knew that He had done just that. I knew that God had a plan for my life and I was facing it as I stood there singing that hymn with the others. What would my answer be? I knew that there could only be one response after all God had done for me.

I returned to work and was approaching my final year's study. Things were going well and I loved every minute I was on duty. The Nurses' Christian Fellowship was approaching the end of its first year and we wanted to have a thanksgiving service to say thank you to God for all His help over the past months. A pastor from a local church was booked to speak and invitations went out to all the staff who worked at the hospital. Feeling very nervous and praying that some would at least come, we were there early to prepare. I have never been more flabbergasted in all my life. We held it in the outpatients department where there were lots of chairs, and not only were they all occupied but folk were standing up all around in every space available.

Matron came as did many other senior sisters and, horror of horrors, I was made to sit on a chair at the place reserved for the guests of honour and my protests counted for nothing. I felt like a fish out of water sitting amongst the elite, which was not what I had intended at all! Far from it! However, others thought differently.

It was a wonderful message on the Good Shepherd and no one could have been in any doubt about God's love for them. God's Son, the Lord Jesus Christ, came to this earth to seek and to save those who have strayed away like lost sheep. His amazing sacrifice of Himself on the cross to pay the price which alone could redeem them and bring them back to God was clearly presented.

From somewhere two beautiful bouquets of flowers were produced, where they came from, I will never know, for I did not think to order any. One was for Matron and one for me. I was so emotional that I could hardly say 'Thank you.' How God blessed that fellowship and spoke so clearly to me that I could trust Him and count on Him whatever the circumstances!

Learning to trust God in every situation

One day towards the end of my second year of training I again stood, knees trembling violently, outside the door to Matron's office. No, thankfully, I had not been summoned—I was there with what seemed to be a very silly request! I had heard about a group of young people who were taking Bibles and Christian literature into different countries. A young American man called George Verwer had a vision for taking the 'Good News' into countries where there were few or no Christians at all. What an exciting adventure! However, the trip was for four weeks and I only had four weeks holiday for the whole year. With days off, I reasoned I could do it. I prayed, seeking God's will. If He wanted me to go then Matron would give her permission. The Lord had shown me Bible verses indicating that He wanted me to go.

'Come in.' I opened the door and went in.

'Yes, nurse?'

Trembling, I asked, 'Please, Matron, may I take all four weeks of my annual leave in a block?'

She stared at me as if I had taken leave of my senses and demanded to know why I was asking such a silly request. 'You will find twelve months a long time to work without a break and you will not be allowed any sick leave.' She studied me long and hard, and after what seemed an age said, 'All right, nurse, I will grant your request.'

'Thank you, Matron,' and I managed to get out of the room on my very shaky legs, absolutely over the moon!

We were given a cassette tape of phrases in the language of the country we had chosen to go to, phrases like 'The Bible is the world's best book,' and, 'This leaflet will tell you what Jesus has done for you,' together with many others, all in Italian (for Italy was the country I had chosen to go to), all of which had to be learned before we went. There were no phrases about, 'How much are these grapes?' or 'How much is this loaf?' However, enthusiasm built as the time drew near.

At last it was time to set off and I joined a few others awaiting the transport. It was late in arriving. The very old van had definitely seen better days. We and our luggage joined the others sitting on the floor of the vehicle, and as each one got into the transport it sank lower and lower, until it only just cleared the ground. It didn't look as if it would get us to the next town, let alone to France. However, with a lot of prayer and persuasion, the clapped-out old banger got us there. It must have been hard for the folk seeing us off and then returning home, for, as the driver prayed with them before we left he said, 'I don't know if you will see them again, but they are in God's hands.'

We spent four days of prayer and orientation in France and then were put into teams and then on to a truck bound for Italy. However, while in France, the mosquitoes seemed to find me their favourite food. My legs became very red, swollen and painful as I reacted to the bites of these persistent insects. Sitting four days and nights in the truck with my legs down made things a whole lot worse, and by the time we arrived in Italy I could not walk. I was very worried. I would be a hindrance like this.

Our team comprised six people: an American man who was the team leader, a Dutch boy, two Swedish girls, a German girl and me. Getting out of the truck on our arrival in Italy, I couldn't walk and the lads had to help me to the building where we were to spend the night. It looked like an old disused church in the darkness, but we were too tired to care about where we were. We girls crawled into the building and into our sleeping bags and went off to sleep. The lads were in the truck.

Before I went to sleep, I prayed, 'Please, Lord, please heal my legs, as I will be a hindrance to the team and I want to be on business for You. Please let my legs be normal in the morning—please be merciful to me and heal me. Thank You.'

When we woke the next morning, the sun was trying to stream through the windows, but they were so dirty and the whole place was festooned with cobwebs. We just wanted to get outside. We would have had cobwebs in our hair if we had stood up! So we crawled out, as we had crawled in.

I stood up and then remembered my legs. I looked down and they were normal size. No redness and not any sign of mosquito bites remained. How we praised the Lord—He had heard and answered my prayer. I didn't have any more bites at all for the whole trip. How good the Lord is!

Now reality set in. We were in Italy—in the Pescara and Ascoli Perchano area—dirty and hungry, but needing to find water to wash in and sell some of our wares in order to have money to eat. If we didn't sell, we didn't eat! That was great motivation. So we set out looking for a stream to wash in, and then into the town to start selling. With only our phrases to help us, it was not easy. We did manage to sell enough to be able to buy some grapes and share those between us at lunch time, but we found it a lot harder than we imagined it would be. People viewed us with suspicion and I have to admit we were looking more and more disreputable as the days went on.

We drove into the country each evening seeking solitude and a river where we could wash. It is not easy to wash, especially one's hair, in a fast flowing river and keep one's balance.

The local youths were a nuisance and would follow us on their Lambrettas each evening when we went into the countryside. They took a lot of persuading to leave us alone.

The boys met a Christian policeman one day and we were all invited to his house for a meal that evening. Pasta with a mince and veggie sauce. How we thanked God for that dear Christian couple being so willing to share their food with us. That was the only real meal we had the whole month.

We stopped to talk as best we could with some men working in a watermelon field, and they cut one up for us. How lovely that was on a hot dusty day!

We decided to go to some walled villages up in the hills and were dropped off in twos to go in and try to sell the literature to the people there. Then the truck would come back to pick us up again. My partner and I went in and started to talk our phrases to the first ladies we saw, and somehow we got separated. I became aware of a commotion but went on trying to sell to the lady I was with.

She went off and then I saw a large group of people coming towards me. They were shouting and waiving their arms and the Roman Catholic priest was leading them. When I realised they were not happy with me being there, and as they were getting closer, I thought I should leave. I looked for my partner and she was nowhere to be seen. I looked for the way out but couldn't see it.

I started to hurry along the road looking for the exit. The crowd was getting bigger and nearer. I began to run, looking for the way I had entered, but I didn't recognise anything until I saw something I had run past a short time ago. I began to panic as large stones started falling around me. I ran faster and started to pray, 'Lord, help me, show me the way out, please.' The crowd was increasing and they were getting closer and the rocks began falling nearer to me. 'Lord, help me, please' I cried. Just then I noticed a path veering towards the wall and ran down it in desperation, hoping it was the one that would lead me out of the village—it was! How thankful I was to be away from that hostile crowd. Where was my partner, though? Had the truck come and picked her up and left me? Would they come back? Yes, they did. We didn't go into any more villages after that!

The local youths were getting more and more menacing and we were going deeper and deeper into the countryside to avoid their finding our parking spot for the night. Trying to escape them, however, could have meant disaster for us. We girls always slept in our sleeping bags in the truck but the two lads went calling distance away into the open countryside—if it was dry—and slept under the vehicle if it was raining!

One morning the Dutch boy came to the truck alone, leaving our leader sleeping. When he didn't appear after a little while, we sent him to wake him up. He came running back to say that he couldn't wake him. We all ran to where he was and he didn't look good. He seemed to have had a reaction to what could have been a spider bite on his face, which was very swollen. He was very drowsy and not breathing so well.

What a situation! He was our only driver able to drive the truck, and we were in such an isolated spot that in whichever direction we looked we could see no sign of civilisation at all. What were we to do? It was in the days before mobile phones.

There was only one thing we could do—we could pray. We all knew from experience that prayer worked, having seen how my legs had been healed overnight. We could bring the situation to our heavenly Father in prayer. We looked at the semi-conscious man lying on the ground before us and then all knelt down around him and prayed like we had never prayed before in our lives. God says, 'Call upon me in the day of trouble and I will deliver you' (Psalm 50:15). As we looked at the sick man before us, we noticed that his breathing became deeper and the facial swelling seemed to be reducing. We prayed on until he started to move and opened his eyes. How relieved we were to see the improvement and praised our heavenly Father for answering our prayer.

We stayed where we were for four days and then it was time for us to make the long journey from the south to the north of Italy, to the city of Bologna. We were all meeting up before the long journey over the Alps again.

As we were travelling on a major road to get to Bologna, we girls were sitting in the back of the truck, I with my back against the road side of the vehicle. I suddenly thought, if a lorry was to hit us, I would be in a very vulnerable position, and so I got up and moved to sit on the opposite side. As I sat down there was a bang and a great crack appeared down the side of the truck just where I had been sitting. We looked at each other in amazement. I was so thankful for the warning from my Lord.

Back in France, we reported on our success or lack of it as the case might be and then into the same clapped out old banger that was waiting to take us homeward again. Still almost scraping the road as it struggled along, it returned us safely to our destinations again where worried relatives were waiting for us. What we must have looked like and smelt like I can only imagine, for it was straight into the bath for me and a bonfire in the back garden for my luggage the next day!

As I progressed through the year before me with no further holiday, Matron was watching me closely, I felt sure. I was being called on to work extra shifts and even extra whole nights, and still continue with my normal day. However, God was faithful and kept me healthy and with extra stamina for all that was thrown my way. How thankful I was, though, when my next week's holiday came!

By now, I was into my third year of training and three months on theatre duty loomed before me. Many of my compatriots didn't enjoy their stint in that department, but as I had worked there as a cadet I was quite looking forward to it. I must admit to being a little nervous as this time I would be more involved.

Chapter 7

However, I loved my time in that department. I was so careful not to touch any of the sterile people and trolleys set up in readiness for the pending operations. I learned about the general set of instruments and tried to remember all their names, then all the extra ones added depending what operation was to be performed and noted that it also depended on which surgeon was performing the operation.

They all had their own preferences. One surgeon preferred an 'Allis' tissue forceps while another preferred a 'Lanes' tissue forceps. One had to learn the surgeon's preference, for you were in trouble if you didn't!

There were a lot of instruments. 'How would I ever remember them all?' I said to the sister who was teaching me.

'You will remember when the surgeon has shouted at you a few times,' she said, laughing. What she said was true—you did remember them that way, and if they were thrown across the floor and you didn't have the right instrument, sterilised, ready to put into his hand, you were in trouble.

I was so eager to learn despite my nervousness, and I just loved being in the team who were all working together for the good and wellbeing of the patient, who had put their whole trust in us for a good recovery.

Gradually I was allowed to scrub up, to assist in some minor surgery and then, as I got more used to it, in even bigger cases, although in a very small part. How I loved working in theatre and being part of the team. It was what I wanted to do if I passed my final exams which were looming large ahead of me—and if I was offered a job, of course!

Sundays were cleaning days unless someone needed surgery. What fun we had scrubbing everything until it sparkled. The walls and windows were scrubbed and hosed down together with the mesh that covered the windows to keep any flies and insects out.

Matron worked alternate Sundays and usually came up the drive to go on duty for 11 am. We always watched for her to get to just the right spot, then we hosed the netting over the open window and she always came to dinner with a very limp cap! Naughty nurses!

So, the time came for our final exams, and how very nerve-wracking it was, especially the practical and oral parts. I was sure my partner and I had failed when we lifted our patient up the bed and he decided to help us. Between us, we banged his head on the bed rail, which rattled loud and clear around the examination room. 'That is all, nurses, you may go now,' and the tone of the examiner's voice surely told us that we had failed. Perhaps though, it was to hide her mirth, which she could have been struggling to control.

I'm not sure which is harder, taking exams or waiting for the results. The waiting seemed to go on forever, though the day arrived at last. I was dreading having to open that envelope and I waited for the others to open theirs first. There it was! With shaking hands I took it and tried to open it, and dropped it on the floor! Trying to recover it from all the excited feet was not easy, but once it was safely in my hand again I moved into a corner to open it,

Peacock & Wickett, Ltd.,   *Kidderminster.*

Sister Eunice

fearing the worst. Opening it, I took out the contents and read 'Pass'. I stared at it in disbelief. Pass! What joy and relief! All the study and hard work had paid off. SRN—State Registered Nurse! I could hardly believe it.

Did I have a job, though? Would I be offered one?

Group after passing our exams
(prize giving outside Kidderminster Hospital)

Thrown in at the deep end

A day or two later, Matron sent for me, congratulated me and asked if I would like to work at the hospital, and if I had any preference? I thanked her and said, 'Yes, I would love to work in theatre, please, Matron.' As theatre was not a popular place to work, she was happy to offer me the post. So for the next few years I saw how the theatre operated. I made packs to sterilise, which were used to cover the patient for operation, made and folded swabs, patched gloves, packed drums with towels and swabs to be sterilised. I learned how to sterilise instruments and which ones were needed for each operation, how to set up trolleys for the different operations and how to be the runner and the scrub nurse taking the case.

I progressed to assisting the surgeon and the anaesthetist, and how I loved the work. I had to do my share of being on call if a patient needed an operation during the night. Added to all this were all the different operations as well as surgeons and their preferences. I loved it, though, and revelled in it.

It was all good training for what lay ahead of me. God had a plan for my life and this was excellent training for it. When one of the anaesthetists knew of that plan, he took me under his wing and taught me some of the basics of anaesthetics and trained me in inserting intravenous needles, putting up drips and intubating patients. How all this was going to be needed in the days ahead as I found myself doing some of these very things, when the doctor needed to operate and there was no one else to carefully watch the unconscious patient. I was so grateful for his kindness, but not all the doctors were so kind and nice!

One Ear, Nose and Throat consultant worked in the dark. He had a lamp, which shone onto a headband mirror he wore which magnified the light. He never spoke but expected the right instrument to be put into his hand. If it was the wrong one, he would throw it across the floor and hold out his hand again, and it was good if you had the right one to replace it. Trying to find the instrument in the dark was quite tricky.

When doing sinus wash-outs, he had a glass container full of warm water hung up on a drip stand and you had to stand on a chair to refill it. One day whilst stood on the chair to refill it, the nurse couldn't see too well in the dark and poured the water all over him. She was just horrified as he turned, looked up at her and said 'Nuuurse' in a deep, gruff voice and then went on with the case. He was not amused—but we were! How I loved my job!

However, I had a call to Matron's office. 'Nurse, I want you to set up and run an endoscopy unit.'

'Oh, Matron, is there no one else?' I said.

'No, Nurse, I want you to do it.'

Endoscopes! How we all hated them. The bulb worked when you checked it, but never when the consultant picked it up. They were the bane of our lives.

The unit was in another part of the hospital—in a separate building. I did like not being on call, and now I was working Monday to Friday 7.30am to 5pm and every weekend off-duty. They were wonderful hours and no 'on call', but to me it was boring and I didn't really like it. As I look back, though, it was all preparation for those plans that lay ahead. For a verse of Scripture kept popping up in the readings from my Bible: '"For I know the plans I have for you," declares the LORD, "plans to prosper you and not to harm you, plans to give you hope and a future"' (Jeremiah 29:11).

After the unit was set up and running for about twelve months, I had another phone call from Matron just before 5 pm at the end of one of my shifts. 'Please come to my office, Nurse.'

'Oh dear,' I thought, 'what now?'

I tapped on the door and entered at her 'Come in.'

'Staff Nurse, Night Sister is sick and I want you to take her place until she is well again.'

What a bombshell! 'I can't do that,' I protested. 'I don't know what she does apart from doing the rounds and giving drugs.'

'Of course you can do it, Nurse. Go home and come back at 7.30 pm and I will give you the report.'

My protests were pushed aside and I had no alternative but to comply. Feeling very nervous, I reported back on duty and she took a large book and opened it to the appropriate page. She proceeded to give me the report on all the most poorly patients and, handing me the keys, said, 'Perhaps you would call in on the Night Sister to see how she is?'

'Where is she, Matron?'

'She is in her flat in Northcliff. Goodnight, Nurse—oh, here's her key.'

I stood staring after her retreating figure with her little dog on a lead trotting after her. Trying to gather my senses together, I quickly read the report again and went to do a ward round on the nearest ward. As I closed the office door behind me, I heard a familiar voice call, 'Nevey, what are you doing here?' It was one of the surgeons with whom I had been working in theatre. 'Night Sister is sick and I am standing in for her.'

She threw back her head and roared with laughter as she headed for the door.

'Well! That's encouraging,' I thought, shrugged and went to do the round with the nurse on the nearest ward.

Chapter 8

Having gone around all the wards, I came back and filled the drug box and headed out to do the drug round. That finished, I wondered what was next, when the bleep went.

'Are you coming to get the keys?' said a rather irate voice. It was the telephonist.

I hurried to her little room. 'What keys are they?' I asked.

'Casualty,' she replied. 'If anyone comes for Casualty, they will ring the bell…'.

'And I will have to deal with them,' I finished!

'Yes,' she replied. 'If the ambulance is bringing in a casualty, they will ring to let you know they are coming. If there are any incoming calls, you will have to put them through to the appropriate wards. There was a pause and then, looking at me, said, 'You can work the switchboard, can't you?'

I shook my head and there followed a short course on how to transfer incoming calls to the various wards. Then she handed me the keys to Casualty—a building just across the yard—and the keys to the hospital main entrance. Putting on her coat, she said, 'Have a good night.'

I looked at the person hurrying down the drive, the locked door and the switchboard and suddenly realised the enormous responsibility on my shoulders. I looked up and whispered, 'Lord, please help me.'

I went back to the office and closed the door, read the report through again, and shut the book. Just then a verse of Scripture came to me: 'Call upon me on the day of trouble and I will answer you' (Psalm 50:15). I claimed that promise as I prayed and sought God's help, then I opened the door and went on with the task before me. Thankfully no one needed Casualty that night but I was kept busy enough. In fact, my feet didn't touch the floor. Not all nights were so 'quiet' though. The weekends in particular could be very lively.

Well do I remember the night of the minibus accident—fifteen casualties, all young men, the worse for having been to a celebration.

There were no serious injuries but each one needed to be checked over by the doctor. With fifteen to cope with, I needed to be organised. I allocated each a trolley, a gown and a blanket. Then I asked each one to get undressed, put on the gown and lie on the trolley under the blanket and then back to patient number one to fill out a casualty card. Down the line I went until I reached number fifteen. He was lying fully clothed on the trolley. I repeated my request and went back to number one. I took his temperature, pulse, blood pressure and pupil reactions and continued down the line to number fifteen. He was still lying fully clothed on the trolley! This time I helped him to undress and put on the gown. I saw him safely on the trolley and put the blanket over him. I put his clothes on the shelf under the trolley and then went to phone the doctor. While awaiting the doctor I thought it wise to check on number fifteen again. There he was, fully dressed with the gown over the top, lying fast asleep on the trolley and covered with the blanket. I undressed him, put the gown on him, covered him with the blanket and took his clothes into another room and shut the door.

When the doctor arrived we started at number one, and on down the line with the doctor to number fifteen. I could not believe my eyes—there had been five dressing gowns on the back of the door. Now he was wearing them all! It took the doctor and me some time to extricate him—they were such a tight fit! His fighting to keep them on didn't help. Fortunately they were all satisfactory and could go.

However, having got into the waiting room area, they couldn't agree and started to shout and fight. I went to sort them out, and as I entered the room a chair sailed over my head. The mention of the police, however, soon had them hurrying down the drive and on their way!

Another night, I was warned by the ambulance crew to expect a patient who had sustained a head injury. A man had been hit on the head with a heavy metal object. I hurried to Casualty to get ready to receive him. Opening the Casualty door I wheeled a trolley outside. It sounded as if a fight was taking place in the ambulance as it came up the drive.

The driver stopped the vehicle and rushed to open the back doors. I was amazed to see three burly policemen and the other ambulance man, hot, red faced and dishevelled as they all struggled to control the casualty who was fighting and shouting and totally uncontrollable. Eventually they, together with the doctor and a little help from me, managed to get the poor man in to Casualty.

Needing to be hospitalised for observation, we managed to get him into bed, but he was like a raving madman. I was very concerned when the men went, leaving three females to care for him, a student nurse, an auxiliary and me. He needed temperature, pulse, blood pressure and pupil reactions every fifteen minutes. He didn't take kindly to being disturbed at all, but leaving off the restraint, a gentle voice and soothing touch made all the difference, especially when his wife arrived.

Next morning, none the worse for the ordeal, he was sat up in bed with a cup of tea. He had no recollection of the previous night, but we did and we had the bruises to prove it.

Another patient coming into Casualty could have changed the course of my life completely. This young man, seriously injured in a road traffic accident, was left fighting for his life. The treatment consisted of intravenous injections, which must be given by a fully qualified nurse, which meant I had to give them when I was on duty. They had to be given very slowly, as they were very painful when being administered and giving them slowly minimised the pain. He gradually turned the corner and responded to the treatment.

When he was able to get up and about, he found a piano hidden away, and being very gifted musically played beautifully to us each evening. How we missed the music when he went home! I was working nine nights on and five off at the time and my nights off coincided with his discharge home. When I came back on duty after my nights off, I had a shock.

The charge nurse who worked opposite me was also on duty that night (we overlapped some nights according to the pattern of our shifts) and brought me an invitation for a date with the lovely young man whose life we had fought so desperately to save. As I stared at the beaming face of the man standing before me, so obviously delighted to have the pleasure of being the bearer of such an invitation, a picture of the person we had nursed, with his dark curly hair and laughing brown eyes came before me.

How long I stood staring at the man before me I don't know—one or two minutes perhaps, but it felt like hours to me! The years of my life raced through my mind and I realised that God had been at work through all the circumstances of my life, preparing me to serve him. I saw an eleven year old child on her knees beside her bed, thanking God for His salvation He had given her through His son Jesus, who died on the cross to pay the price for her sin. I saw myself praying, 'Thank You, Father, for sending Your Son, the Lord Jesus Christ, to die for me, taking all the punishment I deserved for all the wrong things I had done. You gave Yourself for me. I give myself to You to serve You however or wherever You will.'

The holiday at Grange-over-Sands ran through my mind, and my pledge to God as I sang the chorus, 'Master I am willing to dedicate to thee, life and talent, time and money; here am I—send me.' God had taken me at my word and I knew what my answer had to be. 'I'm very sorry,' I stammered, 'but I can't.' I turned and hurried away and I was thankful that our paths didn't cross again that night.

Chapter 9

[9] Situation impossible

It did not seem as if Night Sister was any nearer resuming her position in the hospital. I was happy as I was, and I must admit that it didn't even cross my mind until one morning after I had given Matron the report, she offered me the post of Night Sister. I was happy to accept as my monthly pay would increase, meaning more could go into the car fund which was creeping up nicely. It was still a struggle to get to Areley Kings Gospel Hall but, with lifts from kind people, we met with them as often as we could.

Often I was working on Saturday nights but, with lifts, we were able to attend. It was a great struggle for me to stay awake, especially in the quiet periods during the communion or breaking of bread service. Poor Mum was constantly kicking my foot or nudging me with her elbow when she saw I was 'nodding off'. I tried so hard but I was just so tired!

I had been known to sleep soundly all through the day with a pneumatic drill working on the road just outside my bedroom window. I had not even known it was there. It was more difficult to stay awake in the middle of the row of nine nights when I was on duty. I would come off duty, have a meal, get ready for church, and go usually with whoever had free seats in their car.

A dear couple, Mr and Mrs Kilminster, living on the outskirts of Stourport, would come and collect us some Sundays in time for the communion service. With the family service over, they kindly took us to their home for dinner. After a lovely meal, I was sent upstairs to a wonderfully soft comfy bed, heated with an electric blanket—

sheer bliss. Wakened later for tea, and then off to church, we were then brought home in time for me to go to work. Truly they were such kind people—two more of God's dear angels who helped me along the way.

They, in fact, named my first spanking new red Mini car, 'Martha' because, they said, 'she has got to serve.' It was such a proud day when I was able to take the family out in our brand new car. It snowed! That was a new experience to cope with.

What a blessing that little car proved to be! Now we could get to the services at Areley Kings regularly and under our own steam, as well as the ladies' meetings at Norton Gospel Hall.

Things at the hospital just got busier, with more poorly patients to care for, as those with more minor operations, such as removal of an appendix, hernia repairs, vein stripping etc., now recuperated on a ward at Blakebrook Hospital. That hospital normally cared for the elderly people who had no-one to care for them at home and could not afford nursing home care. We still had the more major surgery cases to care for as well as medical cases, children and trauma cases, which kept us very busy. The busier the hospital got, the more I revelled in it, telling myself that it was good experience and that I needed to gain more experience.

At one time, we had three patients with fractured cervical spines (broken necks) who were paralysed from the neck down and needed all the night staff on duty to turn them every three hours. We could come on duty to a patient being nursed on a ventilator on a ward. With only student nurses on the wards, this meant that I or the charge nurse (who worked opposite me), had to care for that patient as well as care for the hospital and casualty.

One night I came on duty to be sent to the board room to nurse four patients on ventilators (life support machines). One we called 'the bird'. It had that name because of two metal arms that came from the back like wings, almost as if to embrace the patient connected to it. We hated it, because it would only work when connected to the oxygen. As soon as the oxygen cylinder was empty, it stopped working.

When I took the report, I asked the sister when the oxygen cylinder had been changed.

'About half an hour ago' she replied.

'That's good,' I thought, 'as I have a little time to play with.'

She left, and I went to the first patient to check all was well and record his observations. As I was doing them, the bird stopped. Hurrying over, I found the oxygen cylinder empty. Grabbing the re-breathing bag, I began using it to breathe for the patient as he could not breathe for himself. Satisfied his colour was good, I ran to the door and called for help. Then, back to the patient to breathe for him again. No help came. I went to the door and banged and shouted and then back to the patient—still no help came. I began to get fearful as one of the other patients was showing signs of needing attention. Then I remembered, 'Call upon me in the time of trouble and I will answer you' (Psalm 50:15). 'Yes, Lord,' I said, and that's what I did. 'Father, I need help, please send someone.'

I ran to the door again, and who should be coming down the corridor but the hospital porter, the very person I needed. He was the only one who could get the oxygen cylinder for me and connect it to the bird.

He raced off down the corridor, his hobnailed boots clattering loudly on the corridor floor. God had answered my prayer and sent just the right person! I thanked the Lord and learnt a valuable lesson that evening.

I was not happy about the risks that were being taken with patients' lives and told Matron so. I challenged her to come anytime, any night, to see the situation for herself, but she would not accept the challenge. One evening held the promise of a quieter night when I came on duty. After the drug round I went to the nearest ward kitchen to warm up a tin of soup while it was quiet. The bleep went before I had opened the tin, to say two patients were coming in from an explosion. I hurried over to Casualty to prepare and could hear the screams from the ambulance as it came down the road to the hospital. I hurriedly prepared a second drip as the screams continued.

The one patient was not badly injured and was sent to the ward. The other was in a shocking state and, after assessment, needed to go straight to theatre. I called in the theatre on-call team for them to prepare, and when the patient was sedated with drips in place took the casualty up to the theatre staff's care. I cleaned up in casualty and went to get myself a coffee, totally forgetting the soup.

The bleep went again before I could make the coffee and I was asked to go straight to theatre. 'Oh dear,' I thought, 'what have I done?' I went up the stairs and went through the theatre doors, only to be greeted by the ophthalmic (eye) surgeon. He told me to get scrubbed up to assist him, as he operated on the patient's damaged eyes, while the general surgery on the patient's body was dealt with by the general surgery team. I had assisted him many times when I had worked in theatre. I protested and said I had all the other patients in the hospital to care for, but he was having none of it: they were not his concern, he said. He stepped between me and the only door I could leave by, and started pushing me towards the changing room. He was so angry, I thought he was going to hit me! I had no option but to obey. I committed the other patients into God's hand, asking Him to care for them and went to scrub up.

I was shocked at the extent of the injuries sustained by the patient and was still scrubbed assisting the consultant way past the time I should have gone off-duty. He would not hear of anyone taking my place until the surgery was complete.

Feeling sick from the smell of burned flesh, and not having had anything to eat or drink for over the past twelve hours and more,

Chapter 9

I had a dreadful headache. How glad I was when I could go home, but I still had to write the report before I left, all thirty to forty foolscap pages of it!

Looking back now, I can see that God wanted me to move on, but I kept thinking, 'I need more experience.' My scrubbing for the ophthalmic surgeon that night must have put an idea into Matron's head! She announced one morning, after I had given her the report that I was not to call the theatre staff if an operation was needed during the night, that I must take the case myself and scrub. I stared at her in disbelief.

'Have I heard you right, Matron, that in future I am not to summon the theatre staff on call, but that I am to take the case and scrub up myself?'

'Yes, Sister, that is correct.'

'Matron, that is not possible, I can't do that. It is putting all the patients at risk in the hospital, and it needs a minimum of two people for theatre. One person scrubbed at the table, the other one as a runner to get extra swabs, etc.'

All my protests were of no avail, and I could see I had only one course of action open to me. 'May I have an appointment to see you later this morning please?'

'Yes, of course, Sister, would 10 am be all right?'

'Perfectly, thank you, Matron.' I turned to leave the office when she said,

'Oh, Sister, was that your tin of soup in the ward kitchen?'

'Yes, Matron.'

'May I remind you, Sister, that you are not to use the hospital gas to heat your soup?'

I went through the door without replying, for I feared she may not have liked what I had to say. I was furious that after all the extra shifts I had worked, and never received a penny for, I was begrudged a bit of gas to heat my tin of soup! I could not believe it.

My mind was made up! I went home, had something to eat, washed, changed and wrote out my notice.

At 10 am I knocked on Matron's office door and entered at her 'Come in.'

'Ah, Sister, what can I do for you?'

Stepping forward, I placed my notice on the desk in front of her. 'I have come to tender my resignation, Matron.'

She went ashen and I thought she was about to collapse. She stared speechless and unseeing at the fire burning in the fireplace before her. Not a word did she utter as the minutes ticked by.

'Are you all right, Matron? Can I get you a glass of water?' Still no response—not a word uttered! 'Matron, I am very sorry, but you have given me no option. What you are asking of me is not possible. I can't be caring for the poorly patients in the wards, tending road accidents in Casualty and scrubbed at the operating table in theatre, all at the same time—it's impossible.'

It was clear she had no idea at all what went on in the hospital at night. She turned to look at me and said, 'I didn't think that *you* would do this to me' (with the emphasis very much on the 'you'). It felt as if she almost spat the word 'you' at me and then she stared towards the fire again. I said I was sorry that I didn't want to do this. But no further thing did she say, and I walked towards the door, leaving my notice unopened still on the desk before her. I was glad that my nights off stretched before me, so it would be a little while before our paths crossed again.

The month that followed was the most difficult I had ever spent at that dear hospital that I loved so much. After a few days my situation dawned on me, for at the end of the month I would be without a job. I took the situation to God in prayer. The next afternoon, Mum came home after she had finished her shift at Blakebrook Hospital where she worked as a nursing auxiliary. She said, 'I've got a message for you from the Matron at Blakebrook Hospital. He says, 'When is your daughter going to ask me for a job?'

I was amazed. I felt so tired and worn out and I was really struggling through my notice, so I took this to God seeking His will and felt I should ask for a post but only for twelve months. I thought that would be long enough to put me back on my feet. So, I phoned for an appointment and was offered the job of Night Sister, starting a week after I had finished at Mill Street Hospital. But I stipulated that it was just for twelve months.

What a difference! I was responsible for the care of the elderly ones, alternating with one other night sister, and working together when our nights coincided. Three rounds each night and then into the office, which was in a totally empty building. Wood and coal were put beside the fire in winter to stock up the fire as we wanted. A kitchen for making beverages also held a supply of bacon, sausages, eggs, tomatoes, mushrooms and bread and butter. What a contrast to Mill Street! My mind went back to Mill Street days when Matron told me off for thinking about using hospital gas to heat my tin of soup!

It was a cushy job—just what I needed to recover from the busyness of Mill Street. I soon began to put on weight, which was not good for me, but I was only 7 st. 11 lbs and almost invisible when stood sideways. I was quite a bit taller in those days too.

In a former life, Blakebrook Hospital had been the workhouse, and one part of the former buildings remained. A few dear people still called it home. It was separate from the elderly care residents that I was caring for and had its own staff during the day as well as at night. The kitchens, which provided meals for all the patients, were in this block.

One person worked caring for the residents at night in this block and also did repairs to the linen and residents' clothing during the night. Thinking how lonely that must be I used to include a visit to that block on the 2 am round.

One night I entered by a different entrance, via the kitchens, and closed the door behind me. I found myself in a large kitchen with two other kitchens—one the meat kitchen going off to one side, and the vegetable kitchen off to the other. I shone my torch around to get my bearings and became aware of a noise—'plu plu plu! 'There is a tap dripping,' I thought, 'better turn it off,' and as I turned my torch beam in the direction of the sound, I stared in horror! I could not believe my eyes, but the whole place was the same. I shuddered and began to back out! The noise I heard was not caused by a dripping tap but by cockroaches falling from the ceiling into the metal sinks below. They were so numerous that they were at least three to four deep as they walked on the ceiling. Needless to say, I retreated more rapidly than I had entered!

The next morning, I told Matron about it, and he assured me that he would deal with it. I went home glad that those cockroaches' days were numbered. When I went on duty that night I was in for a surprise. After he had given me the report, Matron said 'Oh, Sister, I have taken action over the cockroach problem, and I thought you might like to help.' There was a twinkle in his eye as he pointed to a cardboard box in the corner. 'I've bought you a gun.'

I'm sure he went home chuckling to himself. What did I find in the box? A bug spray! I must admit I saw the funny side, too. How glad I was that I did not have to eat meals prepared in that kitchen! I suppose, I thought, 'What the eye doesn't see, the heart doesn't grieve over.'

Plans were under way to make Blakebrook Hospital into the new general hospital, and we could see the evidence of this each night we came on duty. One warm summer night I returned to the office after the first round, with a cup of coffee, and I opened the window because I could hear two noises: one was a humming noise and the other a scraping noise. I listened, trying to make out what they were.

Chapter 9

I finished my coffee and went outside to investigate the noises. It was a lovely, warm, moonlight night and I stood at the door and listened. Going to investigate in the direction of the scraping noise I found a poor hedgehog with his head stuck in a tin can. He was trying to free himself by walking backwards and scraping the tin along the ground, hoping it would come off. However, it was well and truly stuck and showed no signs of releasing the poor creature.

As I stood there, it really tried hard again to free itself, but to no avail. I reached down and caught hold of the can, holding it stable, enabling him to pull himself free. He stood looking at me as I advised him to avoid tin cans in future. He then shook himself as if to get his spines in place, then turned and ambled off in search of a worm.

While outside, I realised that the humming noise had turned into a whining noise and seemed to be getting louder. I began to feel uneasy, as if something was not right. I went in search of the boiler house technician and it didn't take me long to find him. He was actually in the boiler house and I called him outside to listen. He seemed startled and began to run towards the hospital block. Up the three flights of stairs he clattered in his hobnailed boots, going as fast as he could, with me close on his heels. Reaching the top floor, the noise was much worse, and he grabbed a ladder leaning against the wall and said, 'Hold this, and I will try to get through the hole and I hope we are in time.'

He clattered up the ladder as fast as he could with me desperately praying that he could get his body through the hole and would be in time. Somehow he managed to squeeze through and disappeared into the roof space. After what seemed like ages, the whining noise started to subside as I waited anxiously below.

How relieved I was to see first one hobnailed boot and then the other appear through the hole, followed by the rest of the burly stoker. He managed to get onto the ladder and then, ignoring the rungs, just slid rather rapidly, down the ladder, almost knocking me over, and collapsed in a heap on the floor, ashen faced and sweating profusely.

When he could speak he told me that the valve had stuck and there had only been a few minutes left before the whole block would have blown up! I made each of us a strong cup of tea to recover.

🔟 A word from God

It was about this time that another family, Mr and Mrs Shapland, who lived in Kidderminster and also worshipped at Areley Kings, had the same thought as we did of starting a church in Kidderminster. We began to pray about it, seeking God's will. We met at the home of this couple for prayer and Bible study, and a short time later at our house for the morning meeting or breaking of bread service. This saved us from the icy roads in winter and the long traffic jams in summer as people flocked to the town of Stourport through which we had to travel to get to church at that time.

We had heard that the Council was considering building a housing estate on the Birmingham side of the town and went to check the area out. It would be adjacent to Comberton estate, where there were already a good number of houses but no church. This we thought would be ideal, especially if the Council gave the go ahead for the other estate. This became the focus of our prayers.

As the warmer days came, Mrs Shapland, whose name was Mary, and Dolly went to Comberton estate, having noted how many children were playing around. They gathered them together for a Bible story on a large grassy area in the centre of the estate, which they seemed to enjoy. Thereafter, each week a flannelgraph was set up on the back of Mary's car while Dolly went around the estate gathering up the children. The children seemed to love it, with many coming each week to listen and many awaiting their arrival. There was a problem, though, when the cold weather came, for they had nowhere to take them.

Others began meeting with us in our homes for the morning meeting and the prayer meeting and Bible study. Also at our home, we started having missionary prayer meetings, praying for SASRA (The Soldiers' and Airmen's Scripture Readers Association). That was praying for the soldiers and airmen in our armed forces and the people who were called Scripture Readers who sought to be a help to these young Forces' personnel. We had a prayer meeting too for EUSA (Evangelical Union of South America) and UFM (Unevangelised Fields Mission). It was the latter that held my interest! Numbers to these meetings grew and our large lounge was packed with praying people, and when the soldiers and airmen came, as they sometimes did, all chairs being occupied, it was cushions on the floor and sitting on the stairs. It was certainly a packed house and we loved every minute of it.

The Council came to the decision to build what is now Offmore Estate next to Comberton Estate, and Mr Shapland, whose name was Frank, went to see the plans and we were delighted to know that a plot of ground had been marked out for a church. He went to see the Council and registered our interest to put a church on the plot earmarked for that purpose.

By this time the work among the children of Comberton estate was growing and Mary and Dolly, with a few others, organised a marquee to be set up on the grassed area where the children gathered, and there they held an evangelistic tent campaign. In all, four campaigns were held, with numbers growing and coach trips organised to take them on Sunday school outings. When the weather got cold we gathered them in the Cricket Club tea-room.

Negotiations continued with the Council with regard to building a church, and we continued praying that God would give us the land earmarked for the church on Offmore Estate. We also went as a group and stood on the spot and prayed, asking God to give it to us, if it was His will.

Chapter 10

My work as a night sister continued and I settled down and was enjoying life so much I forgot that I was only there for 12 months. But God did not forget! One night I returned to the office after the 2 o'clock round, put the cup of coffee I had made on the desk and, with my cloak still around me, sat in my chair. I picked up my knitting and looked at the pattern as I had just got to a tricky part and didn't want to make a mistake.

I let the pattern drop into my lap as my mind went to disturbing news that we had heard about the Congo that day. I started to talk to the Lord about it, for news had come through about an uprising and many people were being killed. It was the Simba Rebellion. Simba means 'Lion' in the Swahili language which was spoken in that area. The rebels called themselves Lion men and believed they were invincible, especially if they committed the dreadful acts that still make me shudder if I think of them today. People were being killed, especially Christians, missionaries included.

As I was thinking about these things and allowing my mind to wander, I said, 'One day, Lord, I hope to be there, helping those dear people. Won't it be wonderful when I can go.' Just then in the silence, words seemed to ripple around the room like water rippling in a brook: 'I want you to go now,' the voice said! I shot out of my chair, my cloak went one way, my knitting went another and the pattern yet another! I looked all around me expecting to see someone. But no, I was alone in an empty room in a totally empty block. I checked the whole area for pipes—no, no pipes, radiators etc. I checked that all the windows were closed, and they were.

Going back to the office, as I thought about that strange voice that had rippled out the words like water in a brook as it bubbled its way along over the small rocks and into tiny channels, a verse of scripture came into my mind from the book of Revelation: chapter 1, verse 15, where it says 'His (the Lord's) voice is as the sound of many waters' (taken from the older King James Version, which I was more familiar with). As I thought on this, I thought that I would have been terrified at a great noise, but His voice was gentle so that His child was not terrified. The words were gently spoken, yet with power.

I sat at the desk, reached into my bag for writing materials and wrote out my notice to hand to Matron that morning.

So, what was the next step? Only the Lord knew, and it was from Him that I sought guidance. The next obvious step was midwifery—but it didn't appeal to me at all. I knew that I would be expected to deliver a baby, so it was to Ronkswood Hospital at Worcester that I applied, only to get a reply back that they had their full quota for the next intake and so I would have to wait for the next. Now that posed a problem. I would be without work at the end of the month for six months if I had to wait for the next intake of students. 'Lord,' I prayed, 'what am I to do?' I felt that I should leave it in God's hands for Him to deal with.

I could, of course, have gone further afield, but felt I should stay as local as possible to supply the family with transport for as long as possible. Not long did I have to wait. There had been a cancellation, and they could take me. Hallelujah!—'Thank you, Lord'—how God was deepening my trust in Him!

My year at Blakebrook Hospital was at an end—yes, I had been there just a year as I had promised. I had so enjoyed my time there and would be sad to move on. It was hard saying goodbye, but it had achieved its purpose and I was renewed and ready for the next step. Going to my car to go home after my last shift, I rounded the corner of the building and got a shock—I could not believe my eyes! During the night Martha had been decorated with everything 'baby'—nappies hung from every available hanging space, nappy pins, feeding bottles, empty baby milk tins secured to the back bumper to clatter along behind me as I drove home. Good wishes in lipstick on the windows, all decorating my faithful little red Mini called Martha. I glanced quickly up at the windows but could see no sign of the perpetrators, but I knew they were there, all waiting and watching to see what I would do.

I went up to the car and looked admiringly at all their handiwork and opened the door and got in with a cheery wave and smile and drove off, clattering along as if my little Mini had changed into an old armoured truck with caterpillar type wheels. Driving home, I felt so stupid and very conspicuous and hoped people I passed didn't get the wrong idea!

Needless to say, I wasn't sorry to get home and relieve Martha of all her decorations. Now reality set in. I had never wanted to do midwifery, but here I was, about to start training in a few weeks' time.

It was midsummer as I set off to start my first part midwifery course at Ronkswood Hospital on the very outskirts of Worcester. The fields were filled with beautiful wild flowers. Daisies, buttercups, knapweed, clover, lady's smock, vetch, poppies and so many others.

We lived in at the hospital for the six months but were able to go home as often as our duties allowed us. It was strange going from being a night sister in charge of a hospital to being a student again. We little group of student midwives, in those early days, would all be listening for a bell to ring, telling us that a baby was about to be delivered, and we would run just to observe.

Having observed so many and having started our lectures, we were then allowed to deliver babies under strict supervision.

A certain number of deliveries were required for us to be allowed to take our exams. We worked on all the wards, pre- and post-natal, also caring for the tiny premature babies. How I loved these tiny scraps of humanity who would sit in the palm of your hand and yet each one with their own unique personalities! I adored them. The six months flew by and it was exam time again. I was very grateful to have been successful.

The next six months I was to be at Bromsgrove General Hospital Maternity Unit and working on the district which involved delivering the babies at home for the second part of my course. I could live at home as I was to be with the midwife in my home town of Kidderminster. She took me on antenatal visits and with her to deliveries and seemed satisfied for me to do the deliveries alone. If I needed her, I was to call her on the phone—but there were no mobile phones then and not many homes had a telephone. If you needed to call the midwife because there was a problem, help had to be summoned by the only other person present to help (usually the grandmother of the baby being born) and they had to leave you and run to the nearest phone kiosk.

Each week when I reported back to the hospital I had to report that I was having problems, and was taken back into the hospital. I was very thankful to be out of that worrying situation.

My six months were coming to an end, and again exams loomed ahead. How glad I was when they were over. I went home and returned to the hospital for the results. When they came, what a shock—fail! I stared at the paper I was holding in my shaking hands. How had that happened? I had no answer! Perhaps I needed to learn reliance on God alone. Perhaps I hadn't been doing that. I knew that I needed to seek God.

I was in shock—I was hurting. I felt dreadful! Was the door to Congo closing? I must seek God? I headed for the door, stuffing the offending exam result into the envelope, and went into the corridor. Waiting for me was my tutor. She reminded me of what I had gone through over the past few months on the district, and told me that she would put my name to re-sit the exam next time, and she was very confident that I would pass.

Grateful for her advice and thankful that I could re-sit, I settled down to serious study and passed it next time round. It taught me to take nothing for granted and to understand what it was like to fail, as well as to put my all in to what was before me, doing the very best I could.

Life in the fast lane

So, it was on to the next stage, a two-year course at Redcliffe Missionary Training College. It was an all-female college situated on the west side of London in Chiswick. It was a lovely big red brick property situated on the banks of the River Thames, set in lovely gardens right next to Oxford University Boat Club. It was also right under a flight path from Heathrow airport!

We were about thirty students of all ages and abilities but all with our eyes on serving the Lord wherever that might be. It was run by two ladies, 'the Aunts' we called them: Miss Naish and Miss James, both very wise and knowledgeable ladies. There were some other staff members, a cook, a secretary and an Australian lady who was housekeeper, gardener, nurse, and for whatever else we needed she fitted the bill. We were blessed with extremely good lecturers who taught everything from Church History to temperaments. Miss Naish, showing us how to teach a Sunday School lesson one evening, had us all feeling seasick as she finished telling us the story of the big fish swallowing Jonah. It was brilliant.

Three lecturers I remember well. The Rev. John Caiger, or Uncle John to us as we attended his church, was a lovely gentleman and an excellent lecturer. The others were Mr Bendor-Samuel, a Jewish man, who I believe taught church history, and Mr Derek Swann whom I had the pleasure of collecting from and returning to the local train station each lecture day in my faithful little car, Martha.

We students shared rooms, which could be from a two-bed to a six-bed room, which all had Bible names—Bethany, Canaan,

Chapter 11

Cherith, etc. Each term we were assigned a different room and so we certainly had the opportunity of getting on with many different people in close situations. Time seemed to rule our days—up at 6 am, washed, dressed, bed made and room tidied ready for our quiet time from 6.20 till 7 am. Then on to our cleaning jobs till 7.30 am—these were perhaps hoovering and dusting rooms, like the lounge or lecture room, a corridor with a toilet to clean as well. Windows were kept sparkling with vinegar and newspaper.

Each term two of us were assigned to peel the potatoes for dinner, for the thirty students, as well as staff members, lecturers and visitors. It was an enormous mound of potatoes. When it was the turn of my partner and me, we looked at the pile, then each other, and thought—in half an hour?—impossible! We were given potato peelers to use. I had never used a potato peeler before in my life, but I soon learnt. All had to be ready in half an hour, and we did it, too!

At 7.30 am breakfast—you had to be in your place or everyone was standing silently waiting for you. Your face was very red when you had to apologise. It was so embarrassing; you didn't do it a second time!

At meal times you were expected to follow what your host did. Keen eyes watched, and if you made a mistake you were taken 'for a little walk in the garden' by Miss James and you were made

'IT'S ALL GO DEAR!'

aware of your faults! It was good missionary training for when in a foreign land. It could be considered discourteous to your host, not following the protocol, and could really offend. So, one day we found ourselves eating our grapefruit using a teaspoon, and the next, segmenting it and eating it as an orange!

Sometimes when in an unfamiliar culture, strange food—that is, strange to us—would be on the menu, and not to eat it would cause offence. So, we were given battered tripe for tea—it was like trying to eat rubber. We made a valiant effort and battled on, but it proved impossible and they took pity on us and brought out bread and jam. The staff members could not eat it either! How many pieces of half chewed tripe went through the door in pockets, wrapped in tissues etc., we will never know!

We did various outreaches in the area. One was going to 'The Dive', a coffee bar for the youth. It was further into the centre of London but within walking distance and situated in a basement. We served coffee, tea and soft drinks and tried to get into conversation about spiritual things with those who came. It was not my cup of tea at all! We got back to college late, after lights out, but had to leave our smoke-ridden coats on the washing line if it was dry, or in the shed if it was raining, as they reeked of cigarette smoke.

Door-to-door visitation saw my partner and me knocking on a door and having a lovely talk to a lady, when we became aware of shouting from within the property. When it got worse, we asked if we should leave? Oh no, said the lady, that's only my husband, he is a Spiritist! He wouldn't enter into any conversation, and for the lady's sake we felt it better to leave, but she told us 'to come again any time'.

We were also given ladies' meetings to speak at. The text and passage of scripture was given to us, and when it was ready it was vetted by one of the Aunts. On the appropriate afternoon we went together with one of the Aunts and some senior students. When you got back to college, you were called into the office, together with the Aunt and the students who had accompanied you, for a 'post-mortem'. Your lovely little message you were so proud of and had put your heart and soul into, was pulled to pieces and all your faults laid bare! All the mistakes were spelled out, not to make one feel bad but to teach one—one certainly learned that way. For example, I used to say 'somethink' instead of 'something'. It was pounced on! Perhaps a certain mannerism was noted, and you were told about it. Perhaps a habit of keeping wiping your nose, or putting your glasses on and off, could have folk counting how many times you did it, and the message was not heeded at all. It was all done in love and to help you so that you could change. It did leave you feeling a bit battered afterwards! We were shown how to throw our voice so that everyone could hear, even in a large room. It may all have hurt at the time, but you saw the sense of it and appreciated their brutal honesty. It was 'speaking the truth in love.'

We also formed a choir and sang wherever we were invited and we really enjoyed it. There was one church that we did not like to sing in at all, and that was Duke Street Baptist Church in Richmond. It was a very large, beautiful church, but the acoustics were nerve-wracking for our choir. The trouble was that every one of us felt that we were singing a solo. You could not hear anyone else. Our eyes were avidly fixed on the conductor and you followed her closely. We were always told it was all right, but it was scary. Sometimes you would be picked to sing a solo and you could not say no!

I was so privileged and thrilled to sing in a quartet. I sang bass and I loved every minute of it. It took its toll though as I lost my voice for some time. I was put in isolation and told not to use my voice, but every time someone came they asked me if my voice had come back—which amused me, as I wasn't supposed to speak. So had no idea if it had come back or not. After quite some time I was sent to the West Middlesex Hospital where I was told I had burnt my vocal chords! I think it was singing bass!

We were also given a Sunday school to be part of for the term. One term a senior student and I were put into the 'Canal boatman's' Sunday school. They were lovely children and we enjoyed teaching them each Sunday. They aged from about 7 years to 10 years. They were all so good—well, all except one.

A new minibus had been bought and it was decided that our class should go on an outing to the seaside in the new vehicle. I must admit to being concerned about taking a group of children of that age to the seaside. I was more alarmed on the day when it was a man we didn't know driving the vehicle, and also another lady not known to us. I was even more worried when I saw that 'naughty boy' was there too, and running excitedly all over the place. I began to pray very earnestly.

We set off, I in my Mini and my partner in the minibus. The children were not behaving well, all moving to one side when we approached any bend in the road, so all the weight piled on to one side. They so enjoyed it and would not sit down when told. As we approached a large roundabout, I watched in horror as the minibus went too near to the nearside, mounted a steep bank and landed on its side amidst screams from the children. I stopped the car and raced to the revving vehicle, jumped over the petrol pouring from it, and tried to find an entrance into the minibus to get the children out. The windscreen had smashed, the driver was unconscious, cars stopped to help and the police and ambulance arrived.

We were all in shock and we were all taken for a check-up at the hospital, and everyone was all right except for one. You've guessed it—naughty boy had broken his arm.

It was two very traumatised and upset students who returned to college. However, I have wondered often since, did God keep us from a far worse situation if we had arrived at the seaside?

The days were long and busy. We had to be in bed by 9.45 pm and lights out at 10 pm. You were so tired, you were glad to be there. Bath time (there were no showers) was a 10-minute allotted slot on two evenings each week. You collected your things and went to the bathroom, and if the one before you was late, you might not have time for yours, or the one following you missed out. Many folk waited for our free day on Saturday to soak for as long as they wanted. Many students went out for the day, some to places called Virginia Water, Burnham Beeches, Kew Gardens or even to the airport, plane spotting.

Each term we had a day of prayer and fasting, although food was available if you wanted it. We also had an open day where we could invite friends and family. We provided 'eats' and tea and coffee and put on a programme for them.

When the term ended we went home with whole chapters of the Bible to memorise. One Easter we were given Psalms 22 and 24, and I remember another time Romans chapter 8. We had to write it out when we got back for the new term. Not many of us got it perfect.

Worrying news but still forward

My time at Redcliffe was fast coming to an end, and exams were looming before us. How glad we were when they were behind us and we had the results we were hoping for! It was a relief to go home and live at a normal pace—not the daily race of college. On our arrival home we discovered that the Simba uprising had taken a heavy toll on the missionaries in Congo. Many had been killed and at least one was missing.

After I had been at Redcliffe for two years I had quite a bit of catching up to do when I got home, even though I had been able to come home between terms. Now, new people had joined our little group and the Sunday school was flourishing. For a short time a group of us met at the Scout hut on Wilton estate (which was on the other side of town), but we were still looking to the Lord for the plot of ground to be given to us on Offmore estate.

We were pleased to see a community centre being built on Offmore estate, and when completed it was hired for the Sunday School the two ladies had started on Comberton estate and for the morning meeting. The number of children now in the Sunday school had grown tremendously.

While the two ladies concentrated on the children, my mum, Beattie, started visiting the elderly people in the bungalows and flats on Offmore.

Once or twice a week she would knock on doors and offer the *Challenge* newspaper to all who would accept it, seeking to tell them of God's love for them and the Good News that the Lord Jesus Christ died on the cross to pay the price to redeem us from sin. She then returned the following week to see if they would like to continue to receive the *Challenge* newspaper. I remember sitting, folding piles of these newspapers so that they could easily be transported to give to those who wanted them regularly.

As time allowed, she knocked on more doors. It was a real labour of love, as she worked as a home help each day and took on extra duties for a needy lady nearby each evening too. To get to Offmore she had to catch a bus into the town centre and then another one up to Offmore. This was after making sure Granma was all right and having a bite to eat together.

After delivering the papers she repeated the journey home, again by two buses, in time to prepare the evening meal for us when we got in from work. (Yes, I had taken a job at the new Kidderminster General Hospital again.) How she was able to do it I don't know, for her feet were very misshapen. Once when she went into town shopping with me, after a while she said, 'I think I have something in my shoe.' When we took her shoe off and looked, we found her wristwatch complete with metal linked bracelet. How she walked with her poor feet I will never know!

It was thanks to her regular visitation each week that when we could start to gather folk from the estate for the Ladies' Leisure Hour, there were about 80 to 90 ladies who met twice each month. What a wonderful, single handed achievement! The Lord certainly went with her and blessed her effort.

For me, though, what was the next step? As always, it was prayer, seeking God's will. As I prayed, God led me on, giving me wonderful verses of Scripture that I could stand on when Satan, our enemy, would seek time and time again to make me turn back. The road seemed so long, and whenever one part of the training was completed another loomed before me. How much more, Lord? Joshua 1:9 stood out as I read His word: 'Have I not commanded you? Be strong and courageous. Do not be terrified, do not be discouraged, for the Lord your God will be with you wherever you go.' Other verses, too, encouraged me to keep following His leading.

When one who seemed to set himself up over us, acting as a pastor, told me to my face that I was wrong and that God had not called me and that my place was at home looking after the family and that they needed me, this verse of Scripture came flooding into my reading time and time again: 'You haven't chosen me, but I have chosen you and ordained you that you should go and bring forth fruit' (John 15:16).

Many times I 'put out the fleece' as Gideon did, (see Judges 6:11–40) to be certain of God's will, and God graciously answered every time in the affirmative.

When I tried to tell God I couldn't do this, that it was too big for me, He took me to where Moses questioned God about the task God had put before him, being too big for him. God reminded him that He would be with him to help him, and that was His promise to me, too. Every excuse was blown away. 'I want you to go now' was the word which had rippled around the office room at Blakebrook Hospital and that kept coming back to me again and again.

I must admit it was exciting, but it was also scary! What would it be like in Congo? What if the heat would be too much? What if I got sick and I was alone? So many negative thoughts—but knowing that it was His will I would go trusting Him, and I knew He would not let me down.

I felt God was leading me to the same Mission that Ma and Pa Kinso (the Reverend and Mrs Herbert Jenkinson, the elderly couple at the youth camp at Grange-over-Sands, that God had used to call me initially) had gone through, which today is called UFM Worldwide. I still felt that it was where God wanted me to go—the Belgian Congo as it was then.

However, things were not good there. The news about the Simba Uprising was very sketchy and what we did hear made for terrifying listening. People were being horrifically murdered, especially Christians and missionaries.

I contacted the Mission and went to their headquarters in London for an interview. All seemed to go well and the Mission provisionally accepted me. However, new appointees were expected to raise a support team, to show as a sign that this was God's will for us. I was to travel with the Mission's Missionary Secretary, to speak at meetings, where churches had requested a visit to know more about the missionary work being done in different countries where God's love for the people in these counties was as yet unknown. My aim was to tell of the work I hoped to be doing and to raise a team of people who promised to pray for me and/or support me financially, just small amounts or as much as they wanted. Some just a pound a month, others more, but all given with love and very gratefully accepted.

To me, it looked a daunting task. Would I ever reach the amount that was stipulated by the Mission? Considering airfares to get to and from the destination, the living expenses for four years (that was the time each term of service was in those days), it seemed impossible. God was going to prove to me that He was 'God of the impossible'.

Let me hasten to add that I didn't handle this fund, but it went into a fund at the Mission headquarters. It was used for travelling expenses, insurance purposes, my future pension needs, health needs and a small monthly sum put into my account for me to live on and use in my work whilst abroad.

I really enjoyed raising my team of dear supporters, going with the missionary secretary. We went 'flying low' (his words) to the Isle of Wight, where we spent a week telling of the Mission's work, and I telling of my calling and future work in Congo.

I also went to many other churches in my home area and in Birmingham and as far away as London. I always took someone with me, and usually it was Beattie because she tended to worry and I didn't want to cause her any distress, especially as the meetings were often late finishing. People wanted to talk afterwards, and as the church could be some distance away from home it was not wise to travel alone, especially at night. I usually sang a solo at these meetings and would take my pianist, Stanley, with me on these occasions.

On one trip to London, when we were returning home late at night, Beattie, Stanley, and myself, saw a man a little distance ahead. He leaped from the pitch darkness into my headlight beam, frantically waving his arms. There were no lights at all on that road and that was a scary moment in the pitch darkness. He ran to my car door and tried to open it, saying 'I didn't see him, I didn't see him, help me!' Then we noticed a prostrate figure of a motorbike rider on the verge. Stanley ran up the road to a house to phone an ambulance and the police while I went to the casualty. It was too late, we could do nothing, only stay with him until the emergency services arrived.

Another time, Beattie and I were travelling back from London again when we hit a 'pea soup' fog. Knowing that there was a big crossroad ahead that we had to cross, we crept along with the windows down, Beattie looking for the curb, and I for the white lines in the middle of the road. At last the road could be made out and with much prayer we crossed it. Just past the road, it was as clear as a bell!

Yet another time coming back from London I needed petrol but the garage forecourts were closed, every one of them! I had no option but to keep going, and both Beattie and I were both frantically praying that we would find an open garage; but no, not one, and just outside London the indicator was on empty. I knew I had a little bit left, but we were still quite a way from home. God answered our prayers and brought us from London on a petrol tank registering empty! I got home, put it in the garage and next morning drove it to the local garage to fill up. It got to the garage forecourt and stopped. It needed a push for the last three yards—WOW—Thank you, Lord!

The UFM missionaries in Congo were paying a heavy price with their lives and the reports grew grimmer each day. A doctor who had been captured with his family was made to operate on a Simba (a rebel soldier) but then taken before the operation was completed to rejoin his family, only for all of them to be shot and their bodies thrown into the river.

Of one missionary nurse there was no news at all, and it was assumed that she too had been killed. These were all from the district where the Mission worked. It was so very upsetting.

Thinking that I should use the time wisely, I bought a hand sewing machine, planning to make things for my future home—things like bed linen, tablecloths, napkins, place mats—not realising at the time how unwise that was. Most of them never saw the light of day! How could I display such wealth before people who had nothing? They were overjoyed if you gave them a tin can that you had opened to eat its contents for dinner. They had precious little. I didn't realise this at the time and gaily went ahead. One kind lady made all my uniforms, while I made dresses for casual wear. It was all good practice and would come in useful too.

I spent so much time and money in one local haberdashery shop that they grew curious and asked why I was visiting the shop so often. When I told them the reason they very kindly gave me a bolt of material from which to make my curtains.

What! More training?

Gradually my team of supporters grew, and how glad I was when the number the mission had stated was reached and I could start thinking about the next step. As French was the official language spoken in Congo, I would have to learn that before I could go.

The Simba uprising had come to an end, and Margaret Hayes, the missionary nurse who had been missing whom we heard had been held by the Simba's chief man to care for him and his wife should they become sick, was released also. (She has told of that time in her book, *Missing, believed killed*—well worth reading.) She very kindly communicated with me by post and gave me much valuable advice regarding what I should bring with me for living in the African jungle: for example, a very good sturdy, reliable torch, a Sunday dress to make one feel a bit special occasionally, dresses that covered the knee and with the sleeves just above the elbows, no trousers or jeans—I found her advice to be invaluable.

As it was now considered safe to resume the work again, she and a handful of others were allowed to go back, and so then her letters arrived by airmail from Zaire as it was now called.

As my team of supporters was complete, I was formally accepted into the Mission. The next step was to learn French, and I, together with two other UFMers, a lady, Celia, who became a very dear friend, and a man, H, were all heading eventually for Zaire. Also travelling with us was another lady, who was heading to Burkina Faso with another Mission. She too needed to learn French, and it made sense that we all travel together; and so, when the time came to go to France arrived, I travelled to the Mission HQ in London and spent the night there, meeting Celia for the first time. We got on well from the start.

The next morning we were taken to Heathrow Airport where we all met up and were put on a flight to Paris, where we were to change to a plane to Lyon. Unfortunately my luggage didn't get put on with me, which caused some problems when I arrived. The plane to Lyon was small and we encountered quite a lot of turbulence on the journey. Three of us were fine but M was a very nasty shade of green, poor girl, and I just managed to get a plastic bag to her in time!

With none of us speaking French, we found it hard finding the train station, finding which train to travel on to get to our destination, and getting some refreshments. We knew we were heading for somewhere called 'Albertville' but I had not thought to look it up on a map. Praying much, we boarded a train desperately hoping it was going to our destination, and that we would know it when we got there.

The train went on and on and on and I began to wonder if we had passed it. In those days I used to get terrible migraine-type headaches and I could feel one starting. How I longed to be at the college, but on and on we went. It seemed endless and by now darkness was falling and we could see nothing of the area we were passing through. I began to feel very sick as the headache got worse. 'How much further, Lord?' 'Oh, may we get there soon,' I prayed. We had tried to ask those around us if we were on the right train or if we had passed our destination and they were kind and patient with us and smiled encouragingly, but they didn't speak any English. They just smiled at us from time to time. They kept talking to us in French, but of course, we hadn't got a clue what they were saying.

At last, they, all smiles, made us understand that the next stop was the one we wanted, so we gathered our belongings (or not, as in my case!) and prepared to get off the train. As we did, the cold night air hit us, making us shiver. We waved to our train friends and shouted our thanks in English, but where were we to go now? We had no idea, when suddenly, a young French man addressed us in English—oh joy, someone speaks English! We were soon in his vehicle for the most hair-raising ride of my whole life. We went around every corner on two wheels and I felt so ill that I just wanted to have a couple of painkillers and get into bed.

We had arrived late but a meal was prepared for us. We were met by a Welsh girl who spoke English—what a relief. After a couple of pain relief pills, it was bed, and I've never been happier to lay my head on a pillow!

On waking next morning, I was so relieved that the headache had gone. Going out of my room to go to breakfast, I glanced out of the window and gasped! Wow! I had no idea that we were in the French Alps. What a beautiful sight—alpine meadows with little dwellings bedecked with flowers, framed by snow-capped mountains. I called to Celia to come and look and we stood mesmerised, glued to the spot. It was well worth the long journey to get here. I felt it was so good of the Lord to choose such a beautiful spot for us to learn French.

We were given a few days when we were allowed to speak English but then we could only speak French. We, who spoke no French at all, found this very hard. How much easier if we could hear the word first in English, but it was not to be. Lessons began and we were struggling.

Even though we said we couldn't understand and were struggling, dear Mademoiselle, who ran the school, was sure we would be fine as time went on.

We ploughed on and on to the end of the course which I think was about eight months. I just managed to pass French, but it was never my strong point. We did enjoy that time in the Alps. Celia and

Chapter 13

I walked each day on our time off—up into the mountains where we could hear the cow bells as the cows grazed on the grass, and saw the beautiful alpine flowers, the edelweiss and gentians. We would watch in awe as an avalanche swept down the mountain we just happened to be looking at at that moment.

We also used to walk to an old walled town, Conflans, I think it was called. It was so quaint and beautiful, with the water fountain still working if I remember rightly. One day we went by cable car up the mountain opposite Mount Blanc. It was so fresh and crisp. We benefited from the pure air and felt invigorated. We had to keep to a certain path or we would have been in trouble. Skiers were on the piste on one side, then there was a path for those who were walking, but if you strayed to the other side you disappeared in the deep pristine snow! What a beautiful area it was; I felt so privileged to have spent time there. I would have loved to have been more proficient in French, but time then did not allow for more study because there was still more nursing training to do before I could go.

In Africa I would encounter many diseases that I had never heard of and I would need training to understand them and how to nurse people suffering from them, as well as how to treat them when they became sick. So, I now needed to do a six months course studying tropical diseases at Sefton General Hospital in Liverpool. This time my faithful little red Mini was left at home and I travelled by coach to Liverpool.

It surprised and amazed me how much the landscape changed the nearer I got to the city. From the beautiful green fields of the Worcestershire landscape, with its lovely trees with their colourful blossoms, the hedgerows and verges doing their bit to beautify where they were placed. I could appreciate them so much more seated higher in a coach and not having to watch the road while driving.

The nearer to the city I got, the colour seemed to fade, getting duller and quite drab, the colour almost disappearing altogether as I approached my destination.

It was the time of the troubles in Liverpool and we were warned not to venture out alone. We always went in a group and always carried our umbrellas with us, thankful that the ones with the long metal point on the end were in fashion at the time!

Being there for such a short time, I was surprised that we were given full staff nurse uniforms. Mauve dresses, white starched aprons with purple buckram belts, butterfly caps and two kinds of cuffs! One set was starched very stiffly and were worn when not working and the long sleeves were worn fastened at the wrist. Small, lacy cuffs were worn to cover the rolled up sleeve and hold it in place when working. I absolutely loved it and felt sorry that the time at Liverpool was not longer! All of us on the course wore this uniform, except four Catholic Sisters and two Catholic Brothers who were also on the course. These all wore white coats.

There was a Scottish girl on the course who was also a Christian and we became friends. We all got on very well together, all working on the same unit that was designated solely for nursing people who were suffering from a tropical disease.

As nurses we were used to long and strange sounding words, but these really 'took the biscuit.' We had heard, for example, of malaria before, but now found there were four types, all caused by the bite of the anopheles mosquito. I can only remember two now, quartan malaria and plasmodium falciparum malaria which was the worst one and could lead on to blackwater fever. We actually nursed a patient on the ward who was suffering from that and who, thankfully, recovered.

It was hard trying to remember and spell all the names like kwashiorkor, schistosomiasis, trypanosomiasis and filariasis, the latter caused by the bite of the pepe fly which was the one we encountered in the area where we worked. We all suffered from the flies' bites and could testify to the problems that that brought.

Dengue fever was another disease in our area. It was also called break bone fever, and having had it I can say that it lived up to its name! It was a 'saddle back' fever as it was very bad the first day of the disease, then the next day one felt fine, only to feel very ill and in dreadful pain thereafter until it had run its course.

Let me go back to the patient who had the malaria and blackwater fever that I mentioned earlier. He made a good recovery after being desperately ill and wanted to show his thanks and gratitude to the Scottish nurse and me, for we had nursed him more than the other nurses had. He wanted to say 'thank you' for the care he had received, and invited us to a meal. On the day, he sent a chauffeur-driven car for us.

We began to get worried as the car seemed to be going for miles. Where were we? Should we have come? At last, after what seemed like hours, the car drew up at the entrance to a pub! Our grateful ex-patient greeted us at the door, all smiles, and led us into the bar which was full of people all enjoying a meal and a tipple. As we entered, the room fell silent and all eyes turned to look at us. Our host paused and announced that 'These are the two nurses who had worked so hard to bring me back to health.' Then he led us to a table set for two right by the bar! Every eye was on us! We would much rather have been anywhere else at that moment, but we bowed our heads and said 'thank you' to the Lord for the food and for the recovery, kindness and generosity of the man, standing beaming by us.

The time sped by, and after successful exams it was home again and making preparations to go to Zaire.

My sewing machine and quite a lot of other things I had made and collected were sent to Allinsons, a shipping company in London, to be packed up for the voyage, together with things that I had bought from them I believe, things like mosquito nets, a water filter together with spare filters (or candles I think they were called) and a fridge that ran on paraffin, two Primus stoves, an Aladdin and a Tilley lamp (perhaps it was two) and much, much more besides.

It was all packed by Allinsons into metal trunks, which were crated and banded, and also into metal barrels which were to prove so useful in the days ahead. How grateful I was for the advice dear M gave me regarding all this, as I would have had no idea what to buy or do myself. For example, she advised having the trunks crated and banded because they were easy for thieves to loot if they were not. Certain things were so needed and used, not for what I had thought, but were such a blessing to others as well while I was working in Africa.

It was good to get back on Offmore estate and to see how the work was progressing. We were having the church services and meetings in the new community centre and we continued the missionary prayer meetings in our home.

The problems in Zaire were over and missionaries were starting to return and it was felt that a date for my joining them should be set for September 1970. The church at Offmore arranged a valedictory service in the community centre and many came to wish me Godspeed and every blessing. It was a lovely time and such an encouragement to me, knowing that such a lovely team of supporters were standing with me in prayer as I went at His command. Someone had written out a wonderful poem and a friend gave it to me, which proved to be a very special source of blessing.

'As thou goest step by step, I will open up the way before thee' (Proverbs 4:12, taken from the Hebrew).

> Child of my Love, fear not, the unknown morrow
> Dread not the new demand life makes of thee,
> Thy ignorance doth hold no cause for sorrow
> Since what thou knowest not, is known to me.

One step thou seest, then go forward boldly
One step is far enough for faith to see,
Take that and thy next duty shall be told thee,
For step by step my Lord is leading thee.

Stand not in fear, thy adversaries counting,
Dare every peril, save to disobey.
Thou shalt march on, all obstacles surmounting
For I, the Strong, will open up the way.

Therefore go thou boldly to the task assigned thee,
Having my promise, needing nothing more
Than just to know, where'er the future find thee
In all thy journeying, I go before.

What comfort these words were to me in the days ahead, for there were many difficult times when I cried out to my heavenly Father. He in his faithfulness reminded me of these words, as well as His own precious Word which led and comforted me on so many occasions.

Bumped in Brussels

With passport obtained and all the injections done, it
was counting the days before the overnight flight from
London to Kinshasa where we would catch an Air Zaire
plane to Kisangani. However, I had a problem. My case was more
than the permitted weight and I could not see what I could leave
out! Oh, I thought, why not wear some extra clothes? So that was
what I decided to do. I had the suitcase, my cabin bag, which was
almost as heavy as the suitcase, and my handbag which was bulging
and trying hard not to burst open. I must admit my suitcase closed
more easily but it didn't make too much difference to the weight.
I, however, felt like an advertisement for Michelin tyres!

A dear couple, Mr & Mrs Y, offered to take Beattie and me to
Heathrow Airport to catch my flight, which we gratefully accepted.
I was to travel to Zaire with a seasoned missionary, Olive, who was
returning after her summer break from her teaching duties. At the
airport we were joined by the General Secretary of UFM and the
Missionary Secretary, if my memory serves me correctly. I booked
in for the flight which I discovered was to Belgium, where we were
to change planes for an Air Zaire flight as Olive was travelling on
an Air Zaire ticket. I began to feel uneasy as there was no sign of
Olive and it was approaching the time for us to go through to the
boarding lounge. Anxious glances were cast towards the entrance
doors by all of us and I am sure all were praying for Olive to appear.

Then the flight was called and we were requested to go through,
and I said my goodbyes, but still no Olive appeared! On through

the door into the boarding lounge, a lingering wave, and the door closed behind me. I have never felt so alone in all my life as at that moment. 'Lord, I know you are with me, but I would like Olive as well. Please, please bring her, please.'

I looked around the other passengers and cried out silently to the Lord again, 'Lord, where is she? Please, please bring her.' Those few moments seemed like hours and then we were told to board the aircraft. I picked up my luggage and gave a last look towards the doorway Olive should have been coming through, when suddenly what appeared to be a pale green plastic mackintosh burst through the door, all arms and legs as in a whirlwind, and landed beside me. My face must have been a picture as the occupant, beaming with pleasure and red-faced and gasping for breath, said, 'Traffic was dreadful—didn't think I would make it.'

How glad I was that she did! Never in my life had I been more relieved to see someone than at that moment. We boarded the plane, found our seats and got settled for the short flight to Belgium. We didn't know each other, having never met before, but as sisters in the Lord we chatted as if we were old friends. Soon we were disembarking in Belgium and went to board the overnight flight to Kinshasa, the capital of Zaire. However, we had a shock. We had been bumped! Someone willing to pay more money for our tickets took our seats. We were stranded. No other seats were available and we found ourselves in a 'brown' hotel in Brussels.

It was a room with two single beds. The sheets and coverings were brown, as were the walls and the paintwork, the carpets and the curtains. Early next morning we went to see if there were any cancellations, but no, nor the next day, nor the next. We were praying and couldn't understand why we were having such difficulty.

We went for a walk, and as we were discussing our situation between ourselves we did not notice the well-dressed man walking along the pavement with us. He had obviously heard what we were saying and stopped us to ask us what our problem was. We were soon booked onto a flight that night, for he was one of the important men who ran the airport. Was someone else 'bumped' so that we could get a flight that night? We will never know, but we were amazed at how God had intervened, and that evening we were on our way at last. Why the delay? We do not know, but we know that God has His reasons and perhaps He will tell us one day.

It was a long flight overnight, but I could not sleep. All I wanted to do was look out of the window and catch my first glimpse of Africa. I was glad of the extra clothing for at night it got quite cold on the plane. Eagerly wanting to arrive, the journey seemed to take forever. At last, sunrise flooded the sky and filled it with such beauty.

With breakfast over, we prepared to arrive at the capital city of Zaire, Kinshasa. The plane made a perfect landing, and then, collecting our luggage, we made ready to disembark. The plane door was opened and the tropical heat flooded in. How I wished at that moment that I wasn't wearing so much clothing!

As I got to the door and looked out, what a different world, as I caught my first glimpse of the country I had dreamed about for so long. A shower of rain had just passed over and the tarmac was steaming in the hot sunshine. Struggling with my heavy hand luggage and my bulging handbag, I made my way to the building to check into the country and to collect my suitcase. There was no one there to meet us as we were four days late! Olive was an old hand, though, and soon had everything sorted, and she made sure we were on a flight to Kisangani, the next day I believe. I was amazed at how quickly I got used to the heat once I had taken off all the extra clothes!

The Air Zaire flight the next day was in a smaller plane and I was able to see far more clearly what the country looked like— from above, anyway. We flew over jungle with little villages dotted here and there—just clearings with round leaf roofs covering each little home which comprised of sticks pushed into the red soil, tied together with tough vines from the jungle, and covered with mud and baked hard in the hot sun.

Rivers twisted their way through the land, glinting bright in the hot sun. We flew over the same kind of terrain for mile after mile, but after we had been airborne for two to three hours we became aware of the smell of burning. It was obvious that others in the plane were aware of it by the way folk were looking rather anxiously around. The plane seemed to be flying all right but the smell got stronger and stronger. I looked out of the window but all I could see was jungle—no place to land a plane at all. Olive and I exchanged glances and then started to pray for the Lord's protection.

Suddenly there was a 'whoosh' and a smoking cloth flew out of one of what I thought must have been some sort of heating shaft. It was quickly stamped on and rendered safe by a passenger and the smell subsided, much to everyone's relief! 'Don't worry,' said Olive, 'this is Zaire, you will get used to it!' I can only think that a cleaner had stuffed the cloth that was being used for cleaning into a vent and it had overheated and started to ignite. What was this new land like that I was planning on calling home for the foreseeable future?

We arrived safely at Kisangani airport and the dear ones were there, all smiles to greet us. It didn't matter to them that we were four days late. They were used to life being like this. We were driven to the compound and I learned that I was to stay with Olive in her house there for the time being. After a rest, during the afternoon I got up to find Olive baking cheese scones for tea. Never had anything ever tasted so good!

There were, I think, four properties around a large courtyard secured by big iron gates, made secure by large padlocks. I soon learned one needed to be very aware of thieves, hence bars on the windows which were also covered by mosquito netting, to keep out the mosquitoes in particular but other insects and creatures too.

One property had had the mosquito-netting cut and a long pole used to steal everything that could be got through the bars during one night. It made no difference that the room was protected by ironwork and guards! No one heard anything and neither did the dogs bark!

Opposite the property was a swampy area and we were serenaded each night by the 'bullfrog choir'. It was really fascinating to listen to them—they seemed to have a conductor who started them on the note, then they all came in, as if on cue, in varying decibels of pitch and sound, each one perfectly on its own note; and then, after a few minutes, all ceased at exactly the same moment, as if the conductor's baton was brought down. Some found it very annoying, but it fascinated me.

The road running in front of the property was a dirt road, and each time a vehicle drove past, clouds of thick, red dust filled the heavy, humid air, covering everything in thick dust. I was amazed at how quickly I adjusted to the heat, the humidity and strange sounds. Sleeping under a mosquito net was a must, the zzzzz-ing as the mosquitoes flew around the net at night, seeking entrance, made one extremely glad a net was securely in place.

The church had invited me to work with them before I had left English soil, otherwise I could not have gone, and it was they who had also decided that I should work at the hospital at Bongonda, going there when the new doctor arrived. I was to learn Lingala, which was the language that was spoken in that area. So language lessons began with Del's wife Lois as my teacher.

I was taken by Del, the head missionary who was responsible for making sure all was well for all of us on the mission stations, to register with the authorities. It was locked up with a notice on the door 'Open at 2 pm'. So back at 2 pm we went, only to see a closed sign on the door. So the next day we tried again, only to repeat the previous day's happenings. Four days later we saw an official, but he was too busy then—'Come back tomorrow. I marvelled at Del's patience, but I was assured this was Zaire and I would get used to it. I certainly hoped so!

When I was registered and given my official documents giving me permission to stay in the country, I was free to move from Kisangani, which was the second largest city in Zaire, to a large village called Bangwade about 64 kilometres north from Kisangani, into the jungle. The road from Kisangani to Bangwade was unmade, just a red earth highway from south to north.

In the dry season travelling was a little better as most of the mud holes had dried up and could be traversed, albeit with some difficulty. In the rainy season it was treacherous. Further along that road I have seen holes big enough to cover a bus without the top being visible! Water holes were better than mud holes, at least if water was visible, indicating it had a firm bottom. But if it was mud—beware! Better to check each one though with a good long strong pole before attempting to get through than to regret that one hadn't and find oneself stuck! Sometimes it was best to cut a way around it into the jungle and bypass it totally. I didn't do any driving—I left it to the men!

Bangwade was a large village with a secondary school and a dispensary run by an African nurse. The midwifery side was run by Margaret, the dear missionary nurse who had corresponded with me and been so helpful. She showed me how to cope with midwifery cases that needed a caesarean section operation when no doctor was available to perform the surgery.

For all the sick patients or ladies facing an impossible delivery of their child without surgical intervention, the situation was bleak. At the hospital in town, bribes were demanded from each person they saw, and they were so poor that they faced an impossible situation. So they came to Margaret. They loved her and she loved them, and they trusted her implicitly. It was an honour and a pleasure to be mentored by Margaret. Much I learned not only about midwifery in the African jungle, but many other things which were so helpful, indeed imperative to know, things like how to shake hands. Great offence could be caused if not done with respect. For example, if someone, particularly a chief or elder, offered you their hand, you put your left hand on your right wrist then took the proffered hand, and as you did so you lowered your head in respect. One would do the same for an older person, man or woman, and call them 'Tata' (Father) or 'Mama' (Mother).

Murder! Murder!

Before I went to Bangwade I was taken to meet the church leader Pastor Asani, who welcomed me and thanked me for coming—in French. I was warmly welcomed at the church service on Sunday, even though I didn't have a clue what they were saying as it was all in the local language, Lingala. I tried to make believe I could understand and said a few words in English to thank them. Del interpreted for me.

What I needed now was permission to work as a nurse in that country. So I had to go to the local Zairian hospital and work with the doctor in charge for a short period of time, for him to assess my suitability to practise my profession. It was all in French! He asked many questions as to the prognosis of the patient before us and what treatment was appropriate, and even to assist him during an operating session. I was glad when all that was over and that he was satisfied for me to nurse patients in his country. I was now officially able to practise nursing.

As Lois was pleased with my progress learning a tribal language, she thought I was able to continue alone. So it was decided that I should go to Bangwade to work with Margaret, who had been so kind and helpful in her letters of advice to me. So a date was decided which gave me a couple of weeks longer in Kisangani.

On Saturday afternoons we took a few hours off and went together, taking seats and our tea to a bend in the river which flowed past the town. There were woods to one side, and on the bend of the river a lovely sandy beach where one could paddle or swim if brave enough. None of us were! We were only too well aware of the dangers, but it was lovely to get away from the dust and the noise. I used to look into the woods to see if I would see any wild animals, but I saw none except, one day, I did see a pangolin, a scaly anteater, walking slowly up the road past the Mission property, as if he was heading into town. No one took any notice—perhaps they were used to seeing such creatures walking along the road with them.

Another place we visited was the Wagenia. It was the place where a group of African fishermen had a unique way of catching fish and sold their catch, which was lovely and fresh. That part of the river had a lot of boulders—whether natural or not I don't know. These boulders were the means, so it seemed to me, of holding up timbers cut from the nearby forest and tied together to form a way for the fishermen to clamber along to attend to their fishing baskets. These were anchored to the poles under water where the current swirled so fast through the fishing baskets so that the fish, once captured, could not possibly escape. The men were constantly removing the fish so that the baskets could be filled quickly again, as the rushing current carried the fish into them.

These fishing baskets were, I think, unique to these fishing men of the Wagenia. They were conical with a wide mouth, which allowed fish in but, due to the shape and the rush of the strong river current, the fish could not escape. The men were constantly running over the timbers to empty the baskets of fish and it was fascinating to watch them. I am sure the fish would have been beautiful, as it was so fresh, if one could have afforded the price.

A shopping trip into town for groceries and other items was an experience. Small wooden shops were erected down either side of the road from which blared a cacophony of calypso type music. Tailors sewed their garments on the boardwalk in front of their tiny shops in view of all. I asked for an African dress to be made for me and was amazed that he took no measurements, just looked at me. Come back tomorrow to collect it. I was convinced it would not fit, but it did. I still have it today, but it doesn't fit now!

Mangy dogs looking very much in need of a good meal mooched cautiously about, trying to avoid the eye of all as they searched for anything to satisfy their hunger or of anyone who might clout or kick them!

I bought a bowl and what we would term a baby's bath. It was to be used to do the washing outside on the lawn when I got a little home of my own, and a bucket and other bits and pieces to see me through till my luggage came. What an experience, one had to barter. I watched how it was so expertly done by Lois. The seller asked a ridiculously high price and the buyer responded by offering a ridiculously low price. When you met in the middle eventually, that was the right price. Oh my, I thought, would I ever get used to this strange country? Other things I might need could often be borrowed until my own things arrived. I was amazed when Lois bought me a big sack of flour and one of sugar. I was not used to buying in such large quantities, but, only being able to do a grocery shop about every thee months, it made sense. The flour was a dirty grey colour, as was the sugar, both looking as if they had been swept up from the floor!

With the shopping completed, I was now about to take my first journey into the African jungle as I travelled to Bangwade, 64 kilometres north of Kisangani, I believe. I was excited as we loaded the vehicle and then set off. The town left behind us, we made fairly good progress considering the pot-holed dirt road. The road went through thick jungle, but here and there small clusters of African homes clung to the roadside. As we passed by, friendly people waved and called out their greeting in Swahili. 'Yambo, yambo sana'—hello. Smiling children ran along the roadside with us until we out-paced them.

How fascinating it all was to me, and how hot! It was hard to keep sat on the seats of the vehicle as one slid around, and one had to keep bent to save hitting one's head on the roof for, being further from town, the road deteriorated, with large ruts, deep potholes and, from time to time, holes so large as to swallow the vehicle totally. We seemed to travel a short distance in a long while, but the nearer we got to our destination, the more profuse our welcome.

On our arrival there was a welcoming group of people who crowded around the vehicle, all wanting to shake our hands. Suddenly a group of ladies started singing and dancing 'Yambo, yambo, yambo,' then people shouted 'Karibo, karibo, Mademoiselle, yambo sana.' So many hands grabbed mine, people lining up to shake me by the hand. I was overwhelmed for I didn't expect such a welcoming party.

At last, we went into the lovely little mud brick house shared by Margaret and another missionary for a very welcome cold drink. Bangwade was the home of a large secondary school as well as a dispensary with its trained male nurse, and the maternity unit which Margaret ran. How lovely it was to meet Margaret at last, with her vast knowledge of the Africans and their way of life as well, and she had a wonderful sense of humour.

I laughed until the tears ran down my face as she told us of the night the driver ants got into the chicken house. She acted out how she rescued each chicken from the ant-infested roosting house, handing each one to her companion who picked the ants off as best she could and sat them on the backs of the dining room chairs with their tails over the back of the chair, so that the seats didn't get soiled.

The ants didn't get into the house, as a circle of paraffin was put around the house to stop them. Driver ants will not pass over paraffin, so they would be safe there. She looked so funny as she demonstrated how she leaped from one foot to the other so quickly to prevent giving any ants any possible chance of biting her.

The chickens were left to roost for the night in the dining room and Margaret and her companion went to bed. In the morning they had a shock as the chickens had not understood that they must not turn round during the night, and the chairs needed a good clean before they could be sat on to eat their breakfast of boiled eggs! At least the chickens were saved to lay another day!

I was shown to my little house. Two rooms, a sitting room and bedroom, joining on to another house which was occupied by another missionary lady, overlooking a green lawned area, which I thought would have been very nice to sit on until I came home one day to see what seemed like thousands of baby tarantula spiders running in all directions on it. I was to find later that that lawn was the home of tarantula spiders!

I also had a mafika, or kitchen, built separately at the side. It was round and built up to work-top height, the same as the African houses with sticks and mud, then a chicken wire mesh running around it and finished with a leaf roof. It was adequate for its purpose as it had a wooden work surface all round. My houseboy, Setefano (Stephen) found it adequate to prepare meals for me and even make bread. Yes, I had a houseboy and a gardener. That sounds like luxury, but we were expected to employ both as there was very little work available for them and we were helping at least two families to have an income. It was also well worth it for the beautiful bread the houseboy could make, and for having the area around the house kept clean so that snakes and other venomous creatures could easily be seen crossing over this clear area to enter the property. They could be killed before they could harm someone or even kill a child. So this was a must.

On bread-making day I would watch as I ate my breakfast (I had already been to the dispensary/midwifery with Margaret to see the ladies in labour, or we might have been up all night with a delivery). I would watch fascinated as the grey coloured flour was weighed out and put on a tray and spread out. This was carried to a chair or similar to sit in the hot sun, allowing for all the weevils to pack their belongings and go! Before Setefano proceeded to make the bread, the long-snouted black creatures could be seen making a run for it

while they could. Cool and dark they liked, not light and warmth. It always fascinated me as I watched them making their escape. They all did! For never did I find one baked in the loaf. The bread was delicious and smelt wonderful. I could never wait for the houseboy to go home on bread-making day so that I could cut off a thick crust and spread margarine over it (margarine out of a big tin—we never bought butter as it was rancid when purchased). It was one of the joys of the week—newly baked hot crusty bread—yum, what could be better?

Here at Bangwade we were in the jungle. So, what did I expect? What wildlife? We didn't see anything actually in the village, but I do remember my first night. It was tea time and Margaret and her housemate had invited Del, Lois and me to tea before they returned to Kisangani. As we sat at the table there was a piercing scream. 'What was that?' I thought. There it was again. It seemed louder, as if someone was in real trouble, and then it went again. Surely someone was being hurt—murdered perhaps—but no-one took any notice.

Then I asked, 'What's that?' as it went again. 'What?' they said. It went again and I said 'That.' 'Oh, that's only a hyrax climbing a tree; its screams get higher the higher up the tree it goes.' I listened, and yes, the screams were going higher the higher it climbed. Wow, what a relief, now I could eat my tea in peace! What else would I hear? Bullfrogs in chorus and small furry animals that scream as it climbs trees—what's next? Next, was a honk, honk, honk! That strange noise was made by fruit bats as they helped themselves to breakfast late afternoon—their morning of course.

One afternoon Margaret and I went for a walk and were delighted to see a herd of elephants that had made their way to a nearby river fairly close to Bangwade village, and were thrilled they were there to bathe and drink. They were on the opposite bank of the river to us and I was glad to see there was some distance between us. We were much higher and had a good view. It was lovely to watch them in their natural surroundings.

What high esteem these dear African brothers and sisters had for Margaret. I heard of the welcome she had received when she came back after being held in captivity by the Simbas just a short time before her return to Bangwade. As her vehicle approached the village they were stopped and Margaret told to get out. They sat her in an armchair and carried her shoulder high into the village where a big welcoming committee was waiting with special songs composed in her honour and welcoming speeches.

One afternoon Margaret and I were invited by a group of African men who took us to the river, where we were helped with many extended hands into a dug out canoe. I was terrified, as it was so narrow. We were kept safe and settled into our seats, just a hollowed out trunk of a large tree, and then the men got in and off we went for a trip on the river. They sang at the tops of their voices, many of the songs showing their appreciation for M. The harmonising was just beautiful. I must admit to being worried about the crocodiles in the river, but perhaps they were listening too and appreciating the music as much as we were. Margaret giggled like a schoolgirl from time to time. What an experience! It was a joy to have shared that with Margaret, but I was so glad to get my feet on firm ground again, as I can't swim.

Chapter 16

Operating jungle style

izards were everywhere. One day I went to church taking my small stool to sit on and during the service I felt something crawling on me and it started to come up by my shoulder and I grabbed it and ran out of church for home as fast as I could. Going into the mafika (the kitchen) I bent down below the level of the chicken netting so that no one could see me and grabbed the creature that was screaming in my ear and threw it on the floor. It was a lizard which shed its tail in terror, which wriggled all over the floor. It stood there panting, looking at me. I don't know which of us was more scared! But it took courage and ran away. I got over the scare and went back to church, so glad it was not a snake!

Margaret and I got into a routine so that we both got at least some sleep one night out of every two. Most nights there were babies to be delivered, and usually some premature babies to feed during the night. We split the nights into deliveries for one of us one night while the other fed and cared for the premature babies. The next night we swapped roles, so when it was your night for caring for the tiny babies you at least got some sleep. Very rarely did you get a night in bed when you were on deliveries, or so it seemed to me.

The time came for me to move on, and it was back to Kisangani to prepare for a trip in another direction, this time across country, westwards. The doctor I was to work with was travelling eastwards from the hospital at Nyankunde, to meet us at a large village called Boyulu. The doctor, John, from Northern Ireland was married, and he and his wife Val had a little toddler, Andrew. Almost his first words to me were, 'I've brought some packs and some instruments—can we do some operations?' Ah, I thought, a man after my own heart. 'Why not?' I responded, with a big grin.

That first day I was reminded how these dear folk had suffered in the recent Simba uprising as folk came out of the forest, fear on their faces as if they could hardly believe those awful days were over. The news that a doctor had come was greeted with such joy and delight that overcame their worst fears. I watched as people came towards us wearing bark cloth. It was the bark, stripped off a tree and made soft and supple, I think by soaking in water and then beating with stones or wood until it moved like ordinary cotton or silky material and was quite soft to touch.

They had lost everything they owned, homes destroyed and even their few possessions stolen or destroyed in the uprising. The only way of covering themselves now was to use what resources they could find in the forest in which they lived. How my heart went out to these dear, brave people. It thrilled me to be able help them and I was doing what I loved doing. I was kept busy making sure we had a pack and instruments ready for each case so that the system ran smoothly, and scrubbing to assist the doctor as necessary.

Patients seen by the doctor in the morning were operated on until the light had gone at 6 pm. So it had to be an early start. I loved it. I knew that this was what I had trained for and what God wanted me to do. I think we could have been there for a couple of weeks, perhaps three, and there were some very grateful people left behind when we returned again to Kisangani, where we started our preparations to go and reopen the hospital at Bongonda, the place where the church had decided the hospital should be.

Going around the town, we shopped for bolts of material to make drapes for use during operations, bed sheets and, I think, pillow slips for the hospital wards. How thrilled I was when my crates and barrels came through without harm or tampering. I was going to enjoy opening them when we got there. Bongonda was due north on the same road I had taken to get to Bangwade, only much further on.

With the land-rover packed and with only just room for the doctor, his wife and little boy, and with me in the back, we set off early. We made good time to Bangwade where we had a small break, and then on again, planning on getting there before nightfall. We continued passing small village settlements along the way, where people waved and shouted greetings. In places the road was dreadful and the best way through had to be decided before any attempt was made to pass the great holes that were deep enough to hide large trucks.

Somewhere, about half way to our journey's end, we came to the large village of Banalia. There our journey was halted by the widest river I've ever seen, the River Aruwimi. Islands were dotted here and there and the far bank looked so far away that it was hard to make out anything on the other side. There was a ferry to take vehicles and passengers over to the further bank and at this time could do so under its own steam. (Later we had to take the battery out of our vehicles to power us across, and the ferry had to stay there until another vehicle came on that side to power them back again.)

It was a sizeable village and had a government hospital there. Even though help was available, the prices were too high for the people to afford. While waiting for the ferry to return from the other side, a well-educated European man started talking with us in French. Obviously he was interested in who we were and where we were going. Suddenly an ice-cold coke was put into each one of our hands. Oh, how welcome that was to us hot travellers! How we appreciated his kindness. Never had one tasted so good!

All the passengers had to get out of their vehicles and it was left to the driver alone to safely drive down a very steep slope to the water's edge, where boards were placed from the sloping path up to the deck of the boat. These had to be carefully judged as they went sharply up the gradient to drive onto the boat, which always resulted in the land rover scraping the stone pathway. This was no easy task as a lot of skill was needed by the driver and a lot of power to get the land rover onto the boat which was not too wide. Any transport could easily have overshot the deck of the boat and landed in the rapidly flowing waters.

Val, the doctor's wife, and I were desperately praying that the doctor, land rover and goods would not end up in the water with the crocodiles! Yes, it was crocodile infested! However, he did an excellent job and put the land rover in exactly the right position. Grateful for answered prayer and Doctor John's skill, we walked onto the boat to join him and enjoyed the journey, but we never did see any crocodiles. What we did see was a memorial to the doctor and his family I mentioned earlier who had been taken. Together with his wife and family and two other missionaries they had been shot and their bodies thrown into the river at that very spot. It was a very sombre moment, knowing we were heading to the very hospital where he had worked.

On we went after disembarking, and the roads got no better although the welcome from the villagers grew heartier the nearer we got to our destination. One bit of road we came to was different from all the rest as it seemed to be deeper sand, and I have to admit that I dreaded it. The soil was normally quite sandy, but this one part of the highway, it seemed to me, could cause us problems. It was a stretch of sand where one had to start with the accelerator pedal very well down and, having gained a very good speed, even then we would only just make it through. The land rover was really struggling and almost at a stop as the end of the sand was reached. I always prayed asking for God's hand to be behind us, pushing us along. What a relief to say, 'Thank you, Lord!'

One always had to be on the alert, because there were many dangers to be aware of. Once, as we journeyed along, we saw an enormous snake crossing the highway, one half well into the forest on the left while the other half was still coming out of the forest on the right. What were we to do? Certainly not to get out and look at the creature, so we drove straight over the top! It was so big we all left our seats as we landed with a bump on the other side. We didn't get out or even stop to see if it made it across, but I'm sure it did. On looking back it seemed to be continuing as if nothing had happened.

On another occasion, an elephant herd was crossing the road before us, the bull, an enormous animal, guarding his family as they crossed. We were glad of the distance between us and the massive animal, who didn't seem too pleased that we had come along just at that moment. We breathed a big sigh of relief as the herd disappeared into the jungle. We seemed so tiny and defenceless against this huge beast.

Trees could be blown down in the ferocious storms that came from time to time. One such tree blocked the highway for quite a time while the villagers hacked through it with their machete-style tools. When the road was opened again, the land rover was dwarfed by the enormous bole of the stricken tree.

It was beginning to get dark by the time we got to Kole, a very small village where we had to leave the main highway and take a much narrower path through the jungle. By now it was dark, and this close to the equator darkness comes very quickly. I watched, fascinated, as the headlights picked out our way before us. Where was the road? I could not make it out at all, but somehow our driver found his way, going over numerous log bridges (I think about 17 if I remember rightly), getting out to test that each one was strong enough to take the weight of our laden vehicle.

After what seemed like an eternity (I believe about 11 hours or so) we arrived! I was surprised that we were welcomed by another missionary family from the USA. The man was a builder, just what we were going to need for getting the old ruined hospital back on its feet again. It had suffered dreadfully during the Simba uprising.

Holes were visible where shots had been fired and it hadn't taken long for the jungle to reclaim its territory! He, Tim, and his wife Wanda, welcomed us and had a wonderful meal awaiting us. They had made the doctor's house habitable for the doctor and his family, but I was to stay with Tim and Wanda until my little home was ready. After the meal we didn't stay talking very long as we were so tired after the long journey. I retired to my little bed in a room at the front of the house and slept like a top.

Next morning I met their children and helped to get the breakfast as the houseboy was busy baking bread, and then I went to see where my little house was and what state it was in. Tim was there with the workmen, busy making it habitable for me, but it would be a few weeks before it would be ready. I was so pleased to see that it had a patch of ground reaching up to where I was staying at the moment, suitable for growing things like pineapples, bananas and tomatoes, as well as a chicken house and the ground for the chickens to run on. I was growing excited.

In the afternoon I went to see the hospital. I was thrilled to see twin operating theatres, with the sluice-cum-autoclave room between; also a pharmacy and two wards, one male and one female and, if my memory serves me right, a consulting room. I was shocked at the state of it!

Work people were busy making bricks, ready to do the necessary work. They would be fired in the brick kiln they were making. There was a maternity unit that would have to be sorted out, and further over from the hospital was a leprosarium where the people suffering from leprosy were being treated.

Mingled through the area were the homes of African families—how lovely to see them in their own environment, around their fires cooking the evening meal they had harvested from their gardens. I was fascinated by the beautiful trees and shrubs, among them bougainvillaea—some clothed in lovely red flowers and some dressed in pretty mauve flowers—and jacaranda trees (I think they were) in their blue dresses and what the Africans called flambeau or flame trees—trees dressed in red.

These trees were the home of many weaver birds. These cheerful little creatures, with mainly yellow feathers toned down with some feathers that were more buff coloured, chattered continuously as they built their nests and a few more they didn't intend to lay their eggs in. These were usually on the farthest, weakest ends of the branches, to baffle the snakes who would slide along the branches looking for their eggs or their little ones to eat, only to find these empty nests a decoy and the branch too thin for them to return. The snake would then fall off, usually to be killed by the eagle-eyed people watching and waiting nearby. They chattered among themselves as they busied themselves with their daily living, always with their eyes open for any snake that would dare to raid their

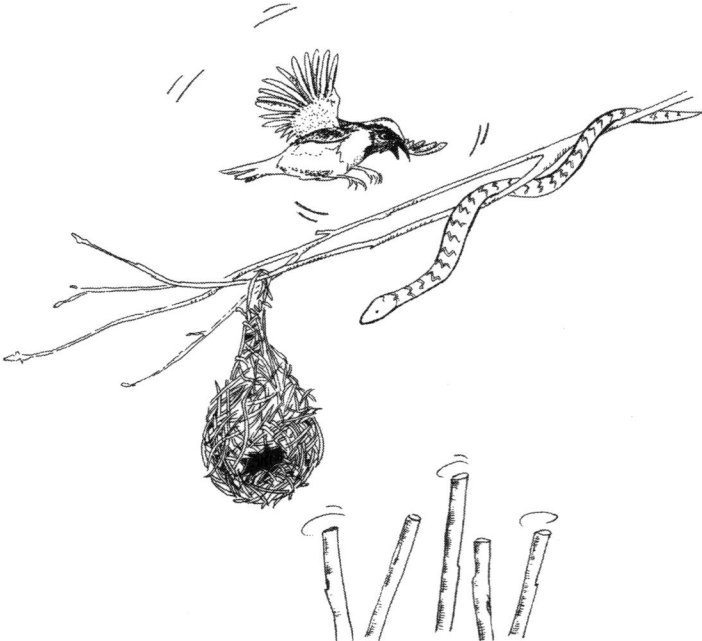

territory. If one did, they would all join in their attack, 'dive bombing' the offending creature, until it made its escape or fell to the ground in the attempt. They built their nests with what appeared to me to be long pieces of grass woven together to form the deep nest with a funnel entrance, lined with moss and feathers. These industrious little creatures were a joy to watch.

The seasons were different from what I was used to. There were only two seasons, a wet season and a dry season. I was fascinated to find that each tree had branches with what seemed to be in different seasons, some branches with new leaves, other with blossom, others with the leaves colouring and others bare! At least, it seemed that way to me. One thing that surprised me was the lack of flowers growing in the soil. I only ever found one, a lantana growing in the garden at the owl-pen, although, one day, two of us were taken into the jungle to see the most beautiful flower that I have ever seen. It was quite large with pink petals but only lasted for one day.

Returning to my new abode, I was delighted to find monkeys playing in the trees next to the house. That, however, was the only time that I saw them. The only other animal that I saw on the station was a large antelope, which walked cautiously from one end of the station to the other, looking nervously around it as it went.

Shortly after we arrived a fierce storm arose one night. It was the first storm since my arrival and I didn't know what to expect. We were all in bed when it started and we saw it well before we heard it. Lightning flashed and thunder rumbled continuously. I had never been in a storm like this! I was scared as it was obviously coming straight at us. The wind started to blow and as my room was on the front of the house, I was getting it full force!

There was only mosquito netting on the windows, no glass, and the curtains caught by the wind stood out from the window at right angles. The thunder crashed continuously with no break in-between, the lightning also flashed continuously, making it as light as midday. I must admit to being scared! No, I was more than scared. I was just terrified! I put my feet over the side of the bed, only to find my flip flops had floated away and the water was up to my ankles. The door opened and Wanda whispered, 'Are you all right?' 'Yes,' I said slipping on my dressing gown.

Together we swept the water out, thankful that the children slept through it. The lightning was still continuous, making it as light as it normally is on a sunny afternoon. We could hear the crashing noises as the trees around us succumbed to the storm, and then it was gone! We made a cup of tea, and thanked God the storm was over and that we were all right. We prayed for our neighbours whose homes were far more vulnerable to storms than ours, and went back to bed.

Next morning, what a sight! We could hardly believe our eyes. The roads were in the form of a square all around the station and the trees had toppled criss-cross over one another, blocking every road. We were so thrilled to learn that not one African home was damaged and no one was harmed. We were so grateful to the Lord. I must admit, that in all the time I was in Africa, it was the worst storm I ever encountered.

We started the task of getting the hospital up and running while the village men cut up the fallen trees. I set about cutting out and sewing the drapes and to make up the packs used while doing the operations, making up the sets of instruments, seeing what was available for any other surgery as well as sorting suture material and getting it sterilised.

It was humbling and exciting to have some of these dear Zairian people come to me clutching something wrapped up in leaves, and with a bow, give with both hands, what they were holding so carefully. (Giving with both hands and with a little bow means the gift was given with much joy and delight and with great respect to the receiver. It must also be accepted with the same joy and delight by the receiver or great offence was caused.) It was perhaps a few phials of catgut and amazingly the glass phials holding the precious suture material remained intact.

Another would come with a surgical instrument or two. 'How did you get these?' I asked, and they replied, 'I took what I could hide when the Simbas came. I took it into the forest and dug a hole and buried it to keep it safe.' Not only did they tell me, but acted it out so well that I could not help but understand. They did not want me to think that they had stolen it. So many things were brought back to the hospital, cleaned up, sterilised and used again. Bless them for saving what they were able to; it was at the risk of losing their lives, too!

We had a generator, which was set up to use for lighting when someone needed surgery during the night. So Doctor John was busy checking and renewing the wiring in the theatres. (They had to be 'Jack of all trades' really.) Until that time we used the Tilley lamps I had brought from home. They gave a good light but did need pumping up from time to time to maintain that good light. However, they did attract all the flying night life that managed to find their way into the operating area, but that couldn't be helped. We made it as secure as possible.

One day I received a message, 'Mademoiselle, the doctor wants you.' He had come through the ceiling of one of the theatres, if I remember correctly, and cut his head. It was soon cleaned and steri-stripped (the edges of the wound held together with tiny strips of plaster) and he was able to continue his repair work!

🔲 Hugged by an eagle

The washing of the instruments used for an operation was done in the little room between the two operating rooms. They were checked to make sure they were clean and the set complete, then wrapped up, labelled and dated. These were then put into the big autoclave to be sterilised, together with other packs, some containing drapes to cover the patient, some of gloves and gowns and things that needed to be sterile for operations, and when full the autoclave was tightly fastened. Three large Primus stoves were lit and placed strategically under it, and when brought to pressure it was held at that pressure for 20 minutes and then the pressure reduced. The packs were then dried and stored until ready for use.

We had some male nurses who had already been trained in Zaire as registered nurses, but until they came I had to scrub up to assist the doctor as well as making sure there were enough packs and instruments available for each case. I was glad when they joined us, releasing me to keep the operating sessions running smoothly.

We also employed a young man to help me with washing the instruments, giving the soiled linen used during the case to the family of the person operated on, to take to the river to wash. When clean and dry, the relative would count each piece back in with the young man, because to keep them was such a temptation. It didn't matter that a goat or two had taken a nibble or a few chickens had walked over it while it was drying, for it was all laid out on the grass to dry!

After a while we got a system working which greatly increased the number of cases we could operate on each day. The trained nurses were taught to give the spinal anaesthetic and open up the site of the operation. The doctor would do the actual operation, and while he was doing that another patient was being prepared ready for the doctor to operate on in the second theatre. The first patient's wound was closed by the nurse while the doctor did the operation on the patient in theatre two.

Meanwhile, theatre one's patient, having been sutured by the nurse, was taken to the ward and patient number three came in to have the anaesthetic given and the wound opened, ready for the doctor when he had completed the operation on patient number two. Before we gave the spinal anaesthetic to the patient, they were always asked if they would like us to pray with them. No one ever refused.

The smooth running of the system depended on us runners. I now had two boys helping me, but it was a herculean effort to keep it running smoothly. A chunk of cake or bread and jam made by my houseboy was a great incentive to keep going. They may possibly have had bread before, but cake, wow! that was something else! How they enjoyed it!

We employed a hospital evangelist, who sought to be a help to the patients and the relatives who came with them to cook a meal and care for them until they had recovered. He held a little service each day for those who came as outpatients, and for the inpatients also, and the Lord really blessed his ministry.

On one occasion I was surprised to see a witch doctor mingling among the patients who had come to seek the doctor's help. He was a tall man, fearful to look at, adorned with animal skins, feathers and bones. His body was painted with dyes obtained from the forest: red, white and black. He looked fearsome and would invoke fear into anyone who met him. I wondered why he was there. Was he sick and had he come for help? Perhaps his own medicine wasn't working! Had he come to see for himself where all his 'patients' were? Had he come to warn us to 'keep off his patch?' I never did find out.

Evidence of his presence could be found if one took a short walk into the forest. A little shrine was not difficult to spot along the roadside, with leaves, bones and flowers decorating the place where an offering of two or three eggs was carefully laid out to appease the evil spirits. They were put there perhaps by someone who wanted success in hunting. I know of one incident where a line of stones, pieces of wood and flowers were put to form a line outside the door of a house. The curse was that whoever crossed over that line first would die. How wise not to make any enemies! This was not the practice of any Christians, let me hasten to add.

By this time, I was in my little home and enjoyed making the curtains for my windows. The local carpenters made my bed and a wooden framed settee and two armchairs. I bought a rush mat locally to cover the cement floor. The kitchen had the wooden crate my trunks had come in and one was turned on its side with a shelf put in to store things like pots and pans, and it also made a good work-top to work on. They also made good cupboards and even a bedside table too!

I used the Primus stove to boil water for twenty minutes, and then the water was allowed to cool before putting it into the filter, after which it went into bottles and was stored in the fridge. It was delicious and hit the spot on a hot day. A bottled gas stove was used to cook food and bake bread which the houseboy used. Setefano had returned to Bangwade as he felt more comfortable living in his own tribe, and so I now had Paulo, who was also the village tailor, as my houseboy from then on.

My bathroom at this time consisted of a room with a chair on which one placed a bowl with some water in. The towel was slung over the back of the chair and the soap sat in a saucer. I put the bath used to wash the clothes in the bathroom and boiled some water in a metal container called a soufferia. Cold water was put in first and then the hot. I could get in and even sit down with my knees under my chin—what a pleasure in such beautifully soft water.

I loved my bath. I might have enjoyed it more, but I had to share it. Let me explain. The barrels in which I had brought my things from home now stood in a row catching rainwater that drained from my roof. This came out of a tap into my makeshift kitchen sink. The water that came from that tap was full of dead mosquitoes as well as a few lesser-known flying insects. To share the bath water with them took the edge off the pleasure—just a little!

My toilet was African style—a big hole dug in the earth with a wooden seat, two round holes cut out, one adult and one child size. It was enclosed with wooden poles let into the ground around it, tied together with vines from the forest and then covered with mud. The entrance was usually a circular corridor with no door. One hung a cloth over the framework at the entrance to let folk know it was occupied. One got used to it, but never to a snake's head looking at you, forked tongue flicking in and out, as it fixed its beady stare on you from the unoccupied hole, nor to the scorpion running up and down the mud wall a couple of feet from you, tail poised to strike! Taking a glance down into the toilet was not advisable either, as it was wreathed with a vast number of cockroaches! The visit was usually as quick an affair as possible.

Our day started at 6 am at the hospital with a short encouraging word from the Bible, and prayer seeking God's help for the day ahead. Then we went back home to have our breakfast. I loved to eat papaya to start (a beautiful fairly big yellowish-orange coloured fruit, filled with black seeds which we scraped out). I loved it with lime juice sprinkled over it. Then about four or five passion fruit, followed by toast the houseboy had made, spread with Blueband margarine from a big metal tin. Sometimes we made jam from papaya, pineapples or guavas, or whatever fruit was available.

While sitting at breakfast one morning I noticed the doctor talking with workmen outside my window. The next moment the doctor, having leaned against the wall, came through to join me as the wall gave way. Termites had destroyed the wall, and I went back to work leaving a big gaping hole in the wall of my house. It was mended by nightfall. I would much rather the doctor had used the door!

Termite mounds could be seen all over the place, and sometimes some of the termites, following a new queen, I think, would take to the air to form a new home for themselves. When this happened, the birds, including the chickens, knew they were in for a good meal! They certainly made the most of the occasion. I could never work out, though, why many of them took to the air only, it seemed, to change their minds, shedding their wings, and returning back home. They knew what they were up to, but it puzzled me, seeing all the wings where they had emerged from the hole. Perhaps though, they were the wings of the ones that were eaten before they had made their getaway?

By now I had some chickens of my own and I did appreciate the fresh eggs they laid. When they were broody I would take the opportunity to increase my flock and put eggs under the hen that was broody, and did quite well with increasing my feathered friends. I kept one very fine rooster, but others that were hatched and reared were for the pot! They made a lovely change from corned beef, pilchards or sardines. There are only so many ways one can use corned beef.

One little hen was a real pet and amazed the Africans. I would call her name and she would fly to me and come to rest on my shoulder, talking to me in her chicken language. They could not understand this at all. Their chickens would run away from them. I had a secret though that they knew nothing about: my little hen's name was 'Peanuts', for she loved them. She knew that if she came then she would be rewarded with her favourite food. No wonder she chortled as she flew towards me. Clever chicken, she even knew which pocket they were in!

I loved my chickens and looked after them well, but from time to time they would get an eye infection, and when it was evening I would take the suffering ones into the house and bathe their infected eyes, put ointment in, and they would heal. They got to know the one that fed them, gave them fresh water and nursed them when sick, provided a safe home to stay in, and locked them safely in from predators each night.

It was lovely to have newly hatched little chickens, fluffy tiny yellow balls that ran after Mom Hen as she cared so beautifully for them. Clucks, meaning, 'I am here, keep close to me,' or a series of fast clucks to encourage the tiny chicken to eat the morsel she had found for it. Also a differing series of clucks that called them all to come and rest for a while under the shelter of her feathers, or the urgency to run to her for protection, when danger threatened, under her strong wings. What a picture of love, of care and of sacrifice, I could see as I watched my lovely chickens.

What a picture to me of my dear heavenly Father's care for me! In Psalm 91:4 I read, 'He shall cover you with His feathers and under His wings shalt thou trust.' How comforting and reassuring I found those words. I too, like those tiny chickens, am loved by my heavenly Father, who keeps me safe from all danger as I listen to Him and trust in Him for protection. Our enemy, Satan, who is described in God's Word as a roaring lion, goes about seeking only to hurt and destroy.

As I mused on this, I could imagine how warm and comfortable those baby chickens would be, cosseted by Mum Hen's soft feathers, and to feel the protection of the strong wing feathers clasping them to her warm body as they listened to the beating of the mother's heart for them. How safe and secure they would feel.

Chapter 17

As I sat there, thinking over these things, I became aware of the frantic clucking of Mum Hen, with the rooster adding his warning as well. This instantly brought me out of my reverie! I knew they were in danger. Jumping up I raced through the kitchen and out through the back door. Immediately I was aware of a distressed Mum Hen sheltering all her brood but one. For one had been struck with fear and it lay spread-eagled on the ground, hugging one leg underneath its tiny body and the other leg stretched out straight below it, looking as if it was forcing itself into the ground trying to hide itself.

As I flew through the open doorway, I landed with my feet either side of the tiny creature, thereby covering it. As I did so, I literally collided with the most enormous bird that I had ever seen—a martial eagle I believe. They weigh about thirteen pounds and six ounces and have a wing span of eight and a half feet! (Or it could have been a fish eagle, but there was no real river near us that I had heard of and I don't remember seeing any white feathers that would have been around its head and neck.) Its huge wing enveloped me, nearly knocking me off my feet. Which of us was the more startled, I don't know, but the predator forgot the tiny chicken and thought only of its own safety and exerted enormous power to get airborne again as quickly as possible and out of danger. There was a cacophony of noise as all the chickens joined in. Roosters from other flocks of chickens added their support, all doing their bit to scare the monster off and to warn of its presence.

The terrified little chicken just lay there, but when the coast was clear, Mum Hen rushed to her little one, with clucks of encouragement and delight. Phew! I needed a strong cup of tea after that and a sit down! As I thought about it, I pondered on how Satan masquerades as an angel of light to fool us. One bird dressed like the others with beaks, claws and feathers could have fooled that tiny chick that it was one of them. He learned early on that that was not the case. I'm sure it would be more on its guard after that, and I realised that I needed to be more on my guard against our enemy, Satan, too.

Most of the buildings on the station were now habitable, but one building that had stood firm and strong was the church which was situated opposite the hospital buildings. It was a large brick built structure with a corrugated sheet iron roof, with quite a few bullet holes in one area which made it unwise to sit directly underneath that part when it rained, unless one had an umbrella! If it rained, it was deafening anyway, for when the tropical rain beat on the metal roof one could hear nothing. There were window holes along both sides, which I believe was a favourite resting-place for leopards on some evenings. No glass or shutters covered these holes.

The seating was bricks or big stones, cemented together to form three series of rows in all, stretching from front to back, with two isles separating them. At the front, steps led up to the raised area where the pastor, or preacher if the pastor was not preaching, and the choir stood, when they were performing. The women sat in the rows on the left-hand side and the men on the right, and children and teens in the middle. Latecomers also sat in the middle if all the spaces were gone. Some people brought their small stools and sat in the narrow aisles or on the floor.

When all the seats were filled, it was 'move along' to get one more or two or three on each row, one sitting forward, and one sitting back, all along the row. It meant a few more could be accommodated. What a squash though, and with the heat too, but it was good fun and camaraderie. Many more filled the window spaces, seating several on each sill. Even so, many more would be crowding around outside. What a wonderful sight to see such huge numbers.

The bell, or the drums, would call everyone to the Sunday morning service. (It was a drum at Bangwade, which could also be used to send drum messages between villages, and a bell at Bongonda.) The services were roughly the same time each week, but when one tells the time by the position of the sun in the sky, timing can't be too accurate, especially on a cloudy day! The services were lengthy, depending on how many had prepared a song to sing. Sometimes solos, quartets and also the wonderful large men's choir. They wrote and choreographed all their songs with all the different parts—yes, the men could get the squeaky notes at the top of the scale, always performed with gusto and sounding beautiful.

Then it was time for the message, which finished when it finished—there was no time set. After that came holy communion, the time when Christians remember the death of the Lord Jesus Christ on the cross, where He gave His life bearing the punishment demanded by a holy, righteous God for the sins we have committed against Him. God's righteous punishment for sin is the death of the sinner. The bread broken represents Christ's body broken on the cross for us, and the poured out wine His blood poured out for us, so by partaking in this service we acknowledge what our Saviour has done in taking upon Himself the sin of each one of us, and thank Him afresh.

What a joy it was to attend a baptismal service. This wasn't held in the church but in a nearby small river with tree-lined banks. We all gathered on the banks, with some climbing trees to get a better vantage point from which to view the lovely occasion. About seventy dear African brothers and sisters witnessed to their faith in the death of the Lord Jesus Christ on the cross of Calvary for them. As they came up from being totally immersed by the water, we all broke into joyfully singing the next verse of the hymn chosen for the occasion. We joined in heartily to begin with, but were rather croaky towards the last few. Not so our Zairian brothers and sisters! They sang heartily and at full volume from beginning to end. I must admit, I kept a wary eye open for any crocodiles that might seek to take advantage of the occasion, but thankfully I saw none.

We missionaries had a time together on Sunday evenings when we had a time of worship in English and a meal together. New folk were joining with us, among whom was one very welcome American nurse midwife. Up to now I had had to deal with all the ladies who came for the birth of their babies. I had discovered one thing. If all was going well with the birth they stayed at home, but if all was not well I would be called to help. Thankfully up until now the doctor had been available to help, but I dreaded the time I would have to cope alone. It was not wise to perform a caesarean section as the woman could well have the same difficulty with the next baby and we might not be there to help! So we performed a small procedure to make the pelvis wider. They didn't understand at all and so stayed much longer than they should in their villages, often resulting in the loss of their baby and sometimes of their own lives too. Now I began to understand why the Lord took me through that difficult time during my second part midwifery.

How I welcomed this new missionary—my little home had been extended either side to make it into a duplex. Caroline, my midwifery comrade, lived in one half and I in the other. In doing the extending, we both had a bathroom and indoor toilet. I even had a shower over the bath—a concrete one; what a luxury! One day, however, I rushed home from work, very hot and sticky and had one thought on my mind: a quick shower. I saw the storm coming and thought I would be in and out before it came, but I misjudged it. Suddenly a flash, a crash and the metal shower was hit as I was holding it. I was the point it earthed, I think, for I felt the current pass through me. I dropped the shower, leapt out of the bath, grabbing the towel, and sat on my bed shaking from head to foot. Caroline had heard the bang and came running round. Yes, I was unhurt, but tears of relief flowed.

It was good to have another single on the station, and we would often eat our tea sat together on a little wall in front of the property. It would be dark by this time and the evening pleasantly warm.

Chapter 17

We listened to the villagers gathered around their fires to eat their evening meal, talking, laughing, children being scolded, dogs yelping as their attempt to steal a morsel to eat was rewarded by a small kick. Some evenings we would ask if we could join them after having eaten our meal. We took our little stools and wore long skirts. Always they made us so welcome.

As we sat on that wall the skies were beautiful, like deep blue velvet, and the stars so big and numerous. We enjoyed finding the Southern Cross and the constellations, and the moon, when full, was enormous, just glorious. But coming back to earth, one particular joy was a gardenia bush just by the wall we sat on, and it was absolutely magical at night. Not only was the smell exquisite, so heady and powerful, but what made it extra special and so beautiful were the hundreds of tiny fireflies that flew around it. Their tiny lights going on and off, it looked like fairyland. We never tired of watching them and enjoying the heady perfume.

I was kept busy at the hospital making up the packs and sterilising them and keeping up with repairing the linen that didn't take kindly to being beaten by stones to get it clean at the river, and patching the gloves used during surgery. It was a constant battle to keep ahead of the needs for each operating list and for any emergencies that came along.

From time to time I was called on to care for one of the female patients where it was not really appropriate for the male nurses to perform the necessary treatment. As I talked with one such lady one morning, I said to her, 'Mama, I can wash away this dirt to make you well again, but only Jesus can wash away the dirt of our sin. Has He washed the sin from your heart?' She shook her head and said that she needed to do that. 'Would you like to do that now?' I asked. Her eyes lit up and she said, 'Oh yes, I do want to do that right now.' So she prayed to the Lord, confessing that she was a sinner and asked the Lord to wash her sin away, forgive her and come into her heart and help her to live for Him. I then prayed with her and I was in no doubt that God had heard and answered her prayer. As she opened her eyes and looked at me, her face lit up with joy. 'Thank you, thank you,' she said. 'I've wanted to do that for so long, but I didn't have the courage.'

That evening, as I sat relaxing after my evening meal, I heard, 'Hodi, Hodi' (That is the equivalent to knocking on the door, but as their doors are made with the same material as their houses, sticks and mud, a knock would not be heard.) Who could this be? I wasn't expecting anyone and I was not on call for the hospital or midwifery. I got up and went to see who was there. It was a man I didn't know.

'Mbote Tata, ojali.' ('Hello Father, how are you?')

I wondered who he was and why he wanted to see me. He asked if I was the one who had spoken to his wife about God today, and I admitted that I was. Oh dear, was he angry? No, he was far from angry. He grabbed my hand and bowed as he told me of how he had prayed for his wife to take that step for so long. He was thrilled! I made tea for us and we had a good chat together. What a joy to rejoice in the wonderful news of his wife's salvation and praise God together in what the Saviour has done for us.

We held meetings for the children each week in the church, each one of us ladies taking our turn. It was not easy to control the numbers that turned up, but the thought that being good brought a treat was an excellent incentive! It was a joy, too, to take my turn telling the story at the children's meeting and speaking at the ladies' meeting from time to time.

All this time I had kept up with language learning but had to be careful not to get mixed up with the Swahili words the doctor used. For example, a greeting in Swahili would be, 'Yambo sana, habari gani?', whereas in Lingala it would be, 'Mbote mingi, ojali malamu?' The day was coming when my skills would be tested. I was to speak to the ladies at their meeting and my teacher, Lois, and one of the senior pastors from the Kisangani church would come to see how I had progressed, and if they were satisfied that I was proficient in the language. Lois was happy to pass me, but the dear pastor said, 'Oh, I was so taken up with the message, that I had forgotten that I was supposed to be an examiner.' 'Oh no, please don't let me have to do it all over again,' I thought; but no, he was more than happy to pass me too. 'What a relief, the last exam behind me,' I hoped!

Going to the hospital one morning, I found everyone in a very excited state! Apparently, the previous evening, the patients and their helpers were preparing to go to bed in one of the wards and were lying in or under their beds, but they had not closed the doors at either end of the ward. A leopard came to the door and looked in and everyone froze! It stepped inside and very slowly started to walk down the ward. It looked at each one as they, hardly daring to breathe, stared back at the beast. Was it hungry? Would it attack? It walked slowly on, stopping from time to time as if trying to make up its mind to understand what they were doing. They all held their nerve, and having obviously satisfied its curiosity, or not fancying any of them for supper, or perhaps not fancying its chances against all the number of people there, it walked slowly on and through the open door at the other end of the ward. A huge sigh of relief went up and I'm sure a lot of praise as they rushed to shut the doors!

I always found it nerve wracking when I had to find my way home in the dark, without my torch, from the hospital or the maternity. It was quite common after a night call-out to the maternity to find a fresh leopard paw print next to the one I had made earlier.

One night I was late leaving the hospital, and it had been a cold, wet and windy day. I had no torch with me, and when I got outside it was dark. I couldn't see the road at all, but could just make out where the church was. So I took my bearings from that. I felt the ground under my feet until it felt like the road, but ahead all looked dark and I could see nothing. I began to feel panicky and disorientated. I started to pray and ask the Lord to guide me. As I did so, I looked up and immediately said 'Thank you, Lord.' Although the sky was dark with cloud and not a single star visible, I could make out a lighter strip of sky between the trees on either side, so looking up, not where I was putting my feet, I made my way safely home. What a lesson that was! I would always be safe if I looked up to the Lord.

However, when I got home, tired, thirsty and hungry, my first thought was to lock up my chickens safely for the night. When I got to the chicken house, however, I found the door had been closed by the strong wind during the day and only about three chickens were safely inside. I groaned. The others had found what they thought were good safe roosting places for the night, but the only safe place was locked up in the chicken pen. Dangers lurked outside—it just wasn't safe. Where were they? Shining my torch around, I retrieved them one by one, and put them safely on the perch.

I kept looking and finding until only one remained unaccounted for, that young rooster I was going to start fattening up for the pot! I shone my torch around and up in the branches of the trees, always making sure that I had a clear run to my open back door. I couldn't afford to let myself be cut off by some dangerous beast. I shivered. 'Oh, where are you, you silly bird?' He was not going to give away his roosting spot easily. Then, yes, there he is, but how am I going to get him from up there. A long stick—that's what I needed. Yes, this will do, and I managed to get him on to the ground. But he had landed farther away from the house and he was well hidden from me and not about to let me know his whereabouts. I knew it was too dangerous for me to go further. I looked around and wondered how many eyes were upon me and who they belonged to. I shivered as I looked around once more. Stray dogs, civet cats, leopards, snakes—no, it's not safe. I had to give up and leave him to his fate. Silly chicken—he knew it was me. He knew my voice and I had even shone the torch on myself so he could see me. It was with a heavy heart that I went through my back door and closed it. His fate came later that night. I heard his cries getting fainter and fainter as some animal carried him off. Each time I remember it, I can still hear those mournful cries.

Jungle joys

It was always so good to get mail from home, and I was blessed with dear ones who packed up biscuit tins with goodies to send through the post to me. What a joy, when someone had been on a shopping trip to Kisangani and brought the mail back with them. On one such trip, I heard the land rover arrive after dark and, grabbing my torch, made my way to the doctor's house where the vehicle had stopped.

One never went anywhere without a good torch that gave a strong solid beam of light. The theory was that it would light up the road ahead and the bush and long grass bordering the road. If a leopard was around, a good solid beam of light shining directly into the creature's eyes would blind it and one could have a chance of escape. What to do if there was another one behind you? We only had one answer to that: pray and run!

I was thrilled to have three biscuit tins and a pile of mail. Joyfully I put one tin on top of another, put the mail on top and secured it by my chin resting on top of it. This was difficult as it was so high and I struggled to see over the top. My torch was in my hand but I couldn't see the road ahead or what was either side of me. I struggled along in the dark with my precious cargo when I stopped dead!

I could hear a deep throaty purring coming from a grassy area to my left. I swung round to face it, shining my torch on the spot, as I did so, the purring noise stopped. Now I was in a dilemma. Only one animal purred that I knew of, a cat. That purr was far too deep and rumbling to come from one of our pets. Could it be a civet cat?

Could it possibly be a leopard? Did these animals purr? What was I to do? If I turned and walked on, it could pounce on me, and that would be that if it were a leopard. One thing was certain, I was not going to drop my precious cargo and run. He could run faster than me anyway. I began to walk slowly backward along the path home with the beam of my torch centred on the spot where the noise had come from. I desperately hoped that if it was a leopard purring in that long grass, the purring meant that it was in a good, happy mood. After what seemed like hours, I at last, got inside my house and closed the door. As I did so, my shaking legs gave way and I sank to the floor, but still holding my precious cargo.

I was rewarded too, as on opening my first box there was a big bar of milk chocolate—it was white, not chocolate coloured as it had been when it began its journey to Africa, but the temperature and atmosphere of the tropics, turned it that way. It didn't alter the taste too much and was thoroughly enjoyed—thank you, dear ones.

One was always wary of what might be around, especially after seeing the fresh leopard paw print next to mine in the damp mud, but other things could be a problem too. If you didn't keep your eyes about you, it would be easy to walk into the trail of driver ants as they went about their business, the soldier ants keeping the column in order as they scurried past with their prey. The first you knew of it would be when a soldier ant's huge pincers on his head sank into your toe … and it doesn't let go. You had to pull the creature off. The body was able to be pulled away quite easily, but the head with the pincers was another story—you lost a small chunk of flesh and the ant lost its life!

We mostly wore flip-flops and this was an ideal target for a small creature that lived in the sand. It was a tiny flea called a 'jigger' and it was, I believe, the female who would burrow into the soft tissue between the toes or around a nail and lay her eggs. You knew nothing about it until it started to itch a little and then get sore, then a tiny black dot would appear and one would then be sure it was a 'jigger.' It was so important to pick out the sack of eggs with a needle without breaking it. If it broke, one could have a nasty infected area, but it seemed to heal if the egg sac was removed unbroken.

Pepe flies were another menace, infecting all of us by their bites as they feasted on our blood. This made us tired through anaemia and we experienced stray aches and pains that we couldn't account for. We were used by them as a host in their life cycle, and all of us had the white thread-like worms moving around in our bodies. As we operated on patients, we would find these worms in the tissues.

One morning one of the nurses came on duty in much distress which was caused by one of these micro filarial worms making its way across his eye. It was quite clear for all of us to see. The doctor was able to put some anaesthetic drops into the eye to deaden the pain, nick the tissue and remove the worm. From time to time we all had a course of treatment to kill them. The tablets made us feel really poorly towards the end of the course, and we were always so glad when it was completed.

Chapter 18

Something else would bug us missionaries but it was not caused by a creature. One could come home and as you got to the door you would groan. The smell was the give-away and the culprit was the fridge! Black fumes would be billowing out and the house inside and every surface was black with the fumes being emitted and smelling horrible.

Our fridges ran on paraffin, or kerosene as the American missionaries called it. Each fridge had a little freezer compartment where a small quantity of fresh meat could be kept. The first thing we would think of was that precious bit of meat that we were storing there for a special occasion.

We lived mainly on tinned things such as corned beef, pilchards and sardines, and a little bit of fresh meat from time to time was a treat. If it was still frozen one would beg a little space in the fridge of one of the other missionaries' freezer compartments if there was room. If not it had to be eaten for the next meal as it could not be wasted and it would not last beyond that.

To solve the problem, the fridge was turned off and the paraffin container removed. The fridge was then turned upside down to rest on its head for a few hours, then it was righted again, relit and one just hoped it would behave and refreeze. In the meantime, one had to clean everywhere to get rid of the black film which had settled on everything, and put up with the awful smell until it had gone.

Not only did we use paraffin to run our fridges but also to light our homes. We used Aladdin lamps. The lamp stood proud off the table with a brass type base and a reservoir for holding the paraffin. A wick came out of this receptacle and a tall slim glass was fitted to it. The paraffin needed to be topped up and the wick needed trimming before it was lit and the glass replaced. It gave a decent light for the immediate vicinity but it didn't light the whole room. This was where candles became useful when moving from room to room.

As soon as the lamp was lit, all the bugs of the night seemed to want to commit suicide in the flame. We found a way around it, though! A small square of mosquito netting mesh kept them from going in. However it didn't stop them from all making a beeline for the light, just when you were busy writing letters or some other task needing the light. Not pleasant as moths and such like got caught in your hair.

There was one creature that didn't go for the light. It had something far more important on its mind. One knew it was there by the noise that it made. When sat quiet writing letters (and there were always a lot of letters to write, especially to those dear ones who so faithfully supported us). One would know of the creature's presence by the noise it made: ZZZZZZZZ. Looking round the room, one could spot it up where the wall met the ceiling. There would be silence for a little while, then it would come back and the noise would start again. ZZZZZZZZ. It was a mud wasp. It was about the size of a hornet and collected little balls of mud to make a nest in which to lay its eggs. The nest was about two inches long and about three quarters to an inch wide. The eggs were laid in the chamber and small spiders and other creatures paralysed and put into the hollow interior with the eggs and the end sealed with more mud. When the eggs hatched, the young would feast on the creatures that the parent wasp had sealed into the nest with them, and when they were strong enough and developed they would break out of their mud home and fly away to start the cycle all over again. The noise was made, by the creature sealing the mud in place with, I think, its tail, but I can't be sure of that.

The Zairians used small hurricane lamps, but they gave such a poor light they usually only used them to travel at night. Their fires gave light, and when the meal was over they went to bed shortly afterwards. When the generator was not working, we used Tilley lamps to see when operating on patients who came to us needing emergency surgery. These used a mantle which was so fragile that it disintegrated easily. It was a pressure lamp that needed to be pumped up quite frequently, because if the pressure went down so did the light! Not the best when a good light was needed to operate by.

There was a tiny shop in the village, which sold a few things needed by the villagers: a large sack of sugar, a dirty grey colour, just like ours was in the sacks we bought from town, just as if it had been swept up from the floor (perhaps it had been) and matches and paraffin. Just the things they would need really.

They had gardens, rotating year by year. The men would cut down the trees and clear a bit and burn the area, the ash making the soil more fertile. The women then took over planting, growing manioc, the root to peel, chop and boil and then pound up with red palm nut oil, making what would almost be mistaken for our mashed potato. The green leaves were boiled and, with a few other bits and pieces added, also pounded into a lovely colourful vegetable dish. Peanuts also added nutrition to the diet, as did tomatoes and 'elephant ears'. The latter was a green plant that when growing started as rolled up leaves, opening as they grew to be as big and in the shape of elephant's ears. Very tasty! Occasionally they would eat meat—a chicken cooked in a delicious peanut sauce with onions and peppers, I believe. They also grew sweetcorn which they would roast in the embers of their fires. I loved their food and would occasionally ask Paulo to cook some 'sombe' for me—the manioc leaves dish.

It was very hard work preparing a meal for the family, and after a very early start all the ladies would go together to their gardens (safety in numbers for there were still dangerous animals around). They would return about three or four hours before sunset to prepare the evening meal. Each one so loaded up, it was amazing to see: huge woven baskets filled with produce, firewood piled on top, and with a baby slung in front using a length of material to keep the child in place. A piece of strong what appeared to be vine from the jungle was placed under the basket. Then another lady would help lift it so that the other end of the vine could be placed across the forehead of the lady who would carry it home, and she would grab the basket, one hand either side of her neck. How they carried it, I will never know.

Greeting the ladies returning from their day in the gardens one afternoon, I said, 'Oh Mama, that looks heavy,' and she promptly put it down and said, 'You pick it up Mademoiselle, go on—go on.' It stood almost as tall as me, and no, I could not move it one bit! I did try very hard. They laughed so much and my admiration for these dear women increased mightily. They have even gone to their garden, delivered their new little baby and still come back with the previous toddlers and their basket laden with produce. The older children would be in school and could be heard all repeating their lessons together after their teacher.

Usually they produced a child every two years or so and they all did their bit to help. Once they had arrived home there was the trip to the water hole to get water, which they carried home in a metal container on their head. Then, fire lit, they could start the evening meal preparation. The next day, it was a repeat performance. They worked so hard; life was very tough for them.

My garden, by comparison, was rubbish as I only had few tomato plants and a few pineapples. I was always delighted to buy pineapples at the door because I would cut off the leafy bit at the top and plant it, thus growing my own. I did have a guava tree but I didn't get much fruit from it. The children raided it before I got there. I'm sure their need was greater than mine.

We did have people come to our doors to sell produce—little tomatoes, lovely until you ate a bitter one. The bitter taste stayed in your mouth for hours, and no matter what you did to try to remove it the horrible taste stayed! It was better to cook them all together and then the bitter taste wasn't noticed.

Eggs would often be brought for us to buy. It was always best to test them in a basin of water in front of the seller, and perhaps one or two of the six they brought to sell would be good.

If a group of children brought them, beware, especially if it was a good number, as they had probably just taken them from under a hen who had been brooding them for a couple of weeks. Bananas, huge heads of them, were often brought for sale, usually green. They were always a good buy as they ripened slowly, and so you were assured of some fruit for breakfast. What a treat to have papaya, passion fruit and bananas after hot buttered toast (or should I say, margarine) for breakfast.

On one occasion I had a tiny antelope brought for me to buy, but that was the only occasion, probably because there was precious little meat on it, not worth cooking for them.

A man came to the door to sell some fresh fish he had caught. I had never seen any fish like it before. Its head was flat and long tentacles came out of it. I did buy it and cooked it but I was dubious about eating it. I offered some to my pet cat and its reaction said it all! It looked at it, tentatively smelled it and then, stepping back from it, shook first one forefoot and then the other and, turning, started to walk away from it. Then turning back it took a long look at the fresh fish I had offered it, then looked long and hard at me, repeated his previous action, shaking first one forefoot and then the other, turned round and walked haughtily outside. I didn't eat it either!

19 Watch your back!

About every three months we went on a shopping trip to Kisangani. We had heard that a new big supermarket had opened. What wonderful goodies would we find? I stayed with my friend Celia whom I had met when we studied French in Albertville. She worked in Kisangani and felt that she needed God's touch upon her ministry.

Each evening we talked and prayed together. I went with her as she went to the local prison and joined in helping with the service. The men were all dressed in the prison jumper, horizontal stripes in mustard and, I think, brown. Some were allowed to go out into town and could be seen mingling with the shoppers. They would return to prison at night and some were in work parties under the guardianship of a warden. When the service was over, several of the prisoners came to shake our hands and to thank us for going.

We went back to her home and began praying and planning for the time we were to spend in a couple of days' time in the local market. Each week she took a table with Christian books, Bibles and helpful literature. She had not had anyone interested enough even to say, 'Hello.'

The market was a flat stoned square with an open drain running around all four sides of it. We set up the small stall and then prayed together for a few minutes. The place was filling up, with most people setting out their wares on a bit of cloth on the ground. The lady next to us had a few tomatoes set out on a banana leaf. Someone else was selling peanuts with a very small tin to measure them out. Another had a few scrawny chickens to sell.

We could tell that some dried fish had been brought for sale. It was called Makiabo. The smell was dreadful and it tasted just like it smelled. I must admit my mind went back to Redcliffe days and the battered tripe when the dried fish was given to me at a meal in an African home. It was hard to say that I enjoyed it, but when I thought of the sacrifice they had made to give the best they could afford, my thanks were very genuine and, yes, I did eat it all.

So folk kept coming until the square was full. It was a cacophony of noise and we both felt nervous and silently prayed for God's help. As Celia's watch said 2 pm, we both stood up and started to sing a duet! As eyes turned towards us, the noise started to abate and emboldened we sang as loud as we could, Celia singing the melody and me the alto. More and more heads were turning towards us and folk were listening. No music to drown the words, they listened right through all the verses and the chorus in-between each verse.

It was all about the grace of God for us, of God sending His Son, the Lord Jesus Christ to this earth to die our death on the cross at Calvary. Our sin has cut us off from the God who loves us and He longs for us to turn to Him to be reconciled. Our sin has alienated us from God and the only path to reconciliation was for a perfect, sinless substitute to die for us. The Lord Jesus Christ is that substitute: none other would do. He is the One God accepts in our place because He alone lived a perfect life that He could offer to God as a sacrifice for our sin.

We sang:

> Wonderful grace of our loving Lord,
> Grace that exceeds our sin and our guilt,
> Yonder on Calvary's mount outpoured,
> There where the blood of the Lamb was spilt.

And the chorus:

> Grace, Grace, God's Grace,
> Grace that can pardon and cleanse within;
> Grace, Grace, God's Grace,
> Grace that is greater than all our sin.

There were several verses to this beautiful old hymn, too many to write here, but they listened silently until we had finished.

As it was a large place and in the open air, we had to sing with all our might, and when it was finished Celia gave a lovely little message as folk left what they were doing and gathered around to listen. It was eight or nine dear people I believe, who trusted in God's grace and mercy and accepted the sacrifice of the Lord Jesus Christ on the cross of Calvary on their behalf. Confessing to God their sinfulness, they asked Him into their lives to be their Lord and Saviour, seeking His help to live to please Him each new day. They came into a wonderful relationship with God, and the joy on their faces said it was real. Perhaps there were others, maybe one day we will know. Our joy knew no bounds as we prayed, and praised God together that night.

The next day was our last in town, and then we were to head back to Bongonda. So that day was taken up with shopping and we went into town in the land rover. Our first shop was for things for the hospital, then on to get things for those left on the station. We went to see what fresh meat was available and managed to fill up a cool box. Then to the vegetable shop and we got a basket that looked more like a flimsy, slatted suitcase and went around looking to see if there was anything that might survive the long journey home. We found a few potatoes, some sweet potatoes, onions, leeks, a cabbage—not much really.

Then, on to the one we were saving till last, the President's new supermarket. Excited, we parked the vehicle and went in. Entering the shop we stood and stared! Every shelf in the whole of the shop was filled with boxes of matches—all stacked so neatly! What a disappointment!

We were glad that the next day was fine as we packed the meat and veggies and other purchases into the vehicle and headed for home. It was the usual bone-shaking journey and we were glad to arrive safely. There were two things we had to deal with as soon as we arrived home: put the meat into the freezing compartment of the fridge and sort through the vegetables.

These vegetables didn't take kindly to the gruelling journey and the green vegetables would have been a slimy, rotted mush the next morning had we had not sorted through them and discarded any looking the worse for wear as soon as we arrived home. From a full basket we only managed to use around a quarter of what was bought. Then it was back to the elephant ears in peanut sauce!

One Sunday morning, I was walking to church with some of the ladies when I noticed a stray dog. The animal was thin and mangy, just sat strangely on the path. It had its hind legs sprawled out before him as its lower back made contact with the ground and its front legs supporting its upper body, which was hunched up in a strange way. Its head, hung down from drooping shoulders, turned slowly from side to side as if trying to make out what was going on around him.

The ladies were watching it closely and seemed on the alert. It got to its feet and started to circle around us. As it got behind me it would have bitten me, but the dear ladies shouted at it, threw stones and tried to chase it away. One lady said to me, 'He is bad, very bad, Mademoiselle.' I looked at the poor animal that was snapping at the air. 'Is he sick, Mama?' I asked. 'Yes, with a bad sickness.' I realised the poor animal was suffering with rabies and if it bit someone or any other animal, the illness would be passed on to them and they would die with rabies too.

We had just lost a lovely little girl, about seven to eight years old, in the hospital, and it had been terrible to watch as the parent sat on the bed behind her, holding her closely by the wrists, with her arms folded across her chest. She, from time to time, struggling to free herself and snapping at anyone within reach, trying to bite them, a wild terrified look in her eyes. Unfortunately they had come for help too late, and treatment could not have helped her. The treatment, a course of injections, should have been started immediately.

I was very grateful to those dear ladies for shooing that poor sick animal away from me that morning, and as soon as I could I told the doctor what had happened, and that a rabid dog was on the loose. He went to the pastor who gathered a group of men together who went in search of the animal. It didn't take long to locate it and put it out of its suffering, thereby saving others from such a terrible death.

One of my tasks at that time was to make up the drug orders brought in by the nurses who worked in the outlying villages. They naturally wanted to get back to their villages as soon as possible. They would plead and cajole for the order to be got ready so that they could be on their way again.

They used various means, one of which was to bring a gift—a couple of eggs or even six if they were really desperate to be on their way. The eggs were usually bad! When laughingly challenged next time they came, they would say, 'They were fresh when I left the village, Mademoiselle, but it was a long way to come.' We would laugh about it, they knowing that I was aware of their ploy.

One day one of them arrived on a bicycle with a goat with a broken leg. 'How did it break its leg?' I asked. Perhaps that was a silly question on my part, for the answer, 'It fell off its bicycle, Mademoiselle,' was just as silly. What could we two singles (for Caroline used to put up their orders as well) do with a goat with a broken leg. Well, the poor leg needed fixing, and so, trying to make sure the bones were in alignment, we put a splint on it to hold it in place.

Chapter 19

We didn't know much about goats, but it seemed to be acting a bit strangely to us. However, we were shocked when a few days later my gardener came running down to the hospital: 'Mademoiselle, Yaka, Yaka noki noki, nyama ajali mabe mingi.' ('Come, come quickly, quick—the animal is very sick.') I hurried home and found Caroline standing a distance from the goat, watching it as it appeared to be in a fit, flailing its limbs and foaming at the mouth. I, of course, couldn't stand and watch. I had to be there to help and comfort. A few minutes later it was dead!

Of course, I told the doctor about it that evening and found myself on the receiving end of a course of anti-rabies injections. How many times in the days ahead, while that course of treatment continued, did I wish I had never set eyes on that poor goat. I reacted to each one of those tiny injections in my abdomen and, before the course was over, Caroline could not find one spot to inject another dose. I went to work supporting my poor red swollen, painful tummy with both hands. I am sure the poor goat did have rabies, as it was snapping at me, trying to bite. Wow! What a present, a rabid goat. I would have preferred rotten eggs!

As time went on, it was decided that an airstrip would be a good idea at Bongonza, so a flattish piece of jungle was chosen and some of the village men set about clearing the site. It would be used by the Mission Aviation Fellowship, or MAF as we called it, to fly sick people to the hospital, as well as equipment and drugs and fresh produce for us from up country. The latter we found a real blessing.

When complete, what a joy to see the small six-seater Cessna plane arrive to test out the airstrip, to make sure it was suitable for use. It circled round, swooping low to cast a critical eye over the site before it attempted to land. When it did attempt to land, it had to be aborted, because a child ran excitedly on the strip of green. However, the third attempt was successful and there was much joy and rejoicing as the pilot stepped from the plane. There was a small area at the bottom end to be levelled more and everyone, especially the children, were warned of the dangers of straying on to the airstrip. What a help it would be, as we were to find out later.

We were usually in our place of service for four years, and then returned home for a period of rest, visiting our supporters and telling about the work we had been doing, showing slides and artefacts, which made it more interesting. It was so good to have a time with family and friends as well, and share with them, for they had sacrificed so much for us. I was thrilled to be reunited with Martha again (the little red Mini that had served me so well). It was graciously loaned to me by the dear friend who had also found her to be a blessing. How I appreciated that kind gesture.

I went back to work at the local hospital for six months to keep up to date with nursing. It did help in one respect, but with hindsight perhaps it would have been better to rest. The church at Offmore was thriving and it was a joy to meet new people. No longer did we have to use the community centre for the services, for sitting proudly on the piece of land where we had stood and prayed that God would give it to us for our church building to be built on, was our lovely church. What a joy it was for me to join with so many new faces as well as dear familiar ones for my valedictory service, for that twelve months had flown by so fast.

'Before they call, I will answer'

It was so good to be back on African soil again. However, one had the feeling that something wasn't quite right. There was an air of change in the country. Things went on at Bongonda as usual and I was now in the small house across the road from the duplex. It was called the Owl Pen. We had a new doctor, Roger, his wife Janet and family, as Doctor John and family were on furlough, as I had been.

One operation we performed more than any other was to repair hernias. It seemed to me that every Zairian had a hernia that needed to be repaired before it strangulated and caused a life or death situation. Every day we had a few cases on the list for operation. I began to wonder where they were all coming from. Doctor Roger did another operation, so needed, which caused people to flock to us: these were cataract operations. So many lives were saved because their hernias were repaired and so many people could be useful members of society because they could see. I felt very blessed to be a blessing to them by having a little part in this.

How thankful the dear people were when they came back to see us, proudly wearing their new glasses. These glasses were old ones that people in this and other countries no longer needed and kindly donated to us. We just had to try them on and test the patient's ability to see through them, and hope they were suitable, as there were no shops where they lived where one could buy or obtain new glasses or even have one's eyes checked.

Everything we needed at the hospital had to be bought in town or shipped from home; a few things could be obtained in Nairobi, but not very much. At one time we were desperately in need of dressings and bandages and nothing was coming through. We cut the bed linen up into strips to be used, but they were soon gone and still no news on what we needed.

There was a Kapok tree in the forest about to shed its seeds, and each seed was covered in kapok, a white cotton-wool-like substance. We gathered the kapok to use as cotton wool, but the woolly covering over the seeds was not very absorbent and didn't make very good cotton wool. So we gave that up.

We were getting desperate and went to the pastor to ask for the church to pray that evening at the prayer meeting and Bible study for the Lord to send us dressings and bandages. We always kept in contact with the mission personnel in town by two-way radio every day at noon, and the next day we were told that some barrels had arrived for us that morning and could we send the land rover to collect them? Although we were not expecting any barrels, we sent the vehicle the very next day. We opened them as soon as they arrived and found they were full of dressings and bandages! 'Thank You, Lord for answered prayer!' 'Before they call I will answer, and while they are yet speaking I will hear' (Isaiah 65:24). They had been sent ten years previously and had been sat in a warehouse waiting for the Simba Uprising to be over. They were just clearing the backlog now that the rebellion was over. What perfect timing! How great and good is our God!

Snakes were not really a great problem but one always had to be on the alert for them. Where you stepped, when you went under trees, one was always aware of the danger. One would often hear a commotion and know that a snake had been spotted. One always looked around a room before entering, and looked in the bed and under it before getting in. A stout stick was always handy, just in case. It was a case of 'I will get you before you get me,' I'm afraid. I hate killing anything, but I had to be wise. If it didn't get me, it might get a child. There were really dangerous mambas as far as I remember.

Going to shower one night while I was living in the Owl Pen, I saw a large scorpion, tail poised ready to get me, running up and down the wall next to the toilet. Oh, that posed a problem, but it had to be dealt with, for I would have been in a great deal of pain if it had got me first.

While sitting on the little wall outside the duplex with C one night, we noticed something on the wall of the 'Owl Pen', my home at that time. We went over to investigate, taking our torches and both of us armed with a stout stick. We were horrified to see the most enormous spider we had ever seen. Its body seemed square and about the size of a tea plate, with stubby legs, the size of one's little finger. We wanted to kill it with a bug spray so that we could ask what it was and all about it, so with both of us spraying it simultaneously, we expected it to fall over dead! But it didn't! It shot under my house, with lightning speed where I had to sleep that night! We both let out the most blood-curdling screams but nobody came to see if we were all right. I was very relieved to have a good sleep that night, but I don't understand how!

One afternoon each week a little group of us went to one of the nearby villages, a different one each week. Our aim was to chat with people, have a singsong if they would like us to and give an encouraging word/message from the Bible. They didn't know we were coming and the place would look deserted when we got there. We were so glad to have Eric and Anne with us because Eric played the piano/accordion beautifully, and when he started to play, welcoming, laughing faces appeared from everywhere. They all gathered around laughing, hands held out in a familiar fashion, left hand on right forearm with the hand extended to shake yours three times in Zaire style, with a small bow, which we, of course, reciprocated. They were always so very welcoming.

From time to time we had a medical student with us to gain experience. One I well remember being with us and staying with Doctor John and family. On one Saturday I had felt a little unwell, and didn't go to church on Sunday morning. Caroline came to see if I was all right and, in spite of my protests, went to get Doctor John. He insisted I go back with him in the land rover and stay with them. During the early hours of Monday morning, I was feeling quite poorly and went to the loo to be violently sick. That's where a bleary eyed medical student found me, in fact almost fell over me, on the floor, hung over the loo. He soon woke the others up and summoned help to get me back to bed. At 7 am I was having my appendix removed. I had excellent care from everyone and made a good recovery. Thank you, Doctor John and Val his wife, Caroline and all others involved, for being there and for taking care of me so well.

That was quite a week. If my memory serves me rightly, someone sprained an ankle by falling through the ceiling of one of the operating rooms. I wanted to see the damage to the ceiling, so went down to the hospital to see for myself (yes, I know it was only a few days after my surgery). Then, as we were all returning to the doctor's house, with me in the lead and with the medical student behind me, another catastrophe! We had to go up a steep flight of eight to ten steps to reach the balcony before the door to the doctor's home. The medical student went past me to open the gate and disappeared through the boards of the veranda into the room beneath. Poor young man—but I was so glad that he had been chivalrous. He himself wasn't hurt, only his dignity. How thankful I was that it hadn't been me!

I have mentioned what occupied the ladies all day, but what of the men? They did clear the new garden patch, and as the seasons were not like ours, just wet and dry seasons, it was wise to take advantage of the rains when they came. When their part in making the gardens were completed they went hunting, using various methods. Sometimes traps were set to ensnare the animal, or a pit dug and covered over so the unsuspecting creature would fall in and could not escape. Sometimes small antelopes were caught and the traps had to be inspected regularly or larger predators might get there before them and steal what they had caught.

They might fish if there was a river nearby, but one had to be very careful of the crocodiles, for they were always on the lookout for a meal, human or otherwise. Once we were invited by the chief of a village to a meal, and a goat had been killed for the occasion. I didn't know quite what to do when I found a piece of meat on my plate, still with the goat's coat on! They hadn't told us how to cope with that one at Redcliffe Missionary Training College!

One afternoon a man was brought to the hospital after being gored through the chest by an enraged bull elephant. The man and his friend were on a hunting trip when they came upon the herd of elephants. The huge animal, thinking his family were in danger, attacked the man nearest to him. The maddened animal thrust his great tusk through the man's chest, just missing his heart, threw him up in the air and stamped on him when he hit the ground. The elephant herd then made off and his friend ran to help him.

They have an amazing way of getting a sick or injured person to medical help. They use a jungle ambulance—two stout branches are cut and the bark removed, then a fishing net hung from them to form a hammock. Obviously this was prepared in advance. The sick person would be laid in it and two men, one at the head and one at the feet, would lift the poles to their shoulders and run to the next village. There, two others would take the place of the runners who would return home, and they would run to the next village with the sick person, and so it went on until the hospital was reached. When they got to the Government hospital at Banalia, the staff there dressed the wound and gave him an injection of penicillin. 'Please don't leave me here,' the injured man pleaded. 'Take me to the hospital at Bongonda. If I can get there, I will be saved.' So the jungle ambulance continued.

However, when he got there, there was no doctor. He had gone to town but was due back later that day. I must admit these dear people are tough. He recovered, but had to make do with one lung. He never went hunting again, but he was saved. Oh yes! Gloriously saved, and all his family.

As time went on, we began to notice subtle changes towards foreigners. We were not as welcome as we once were. For example, walking along the pavement in town, we would be pushed into the road. Attitudes towards us were changing. All seemed well back on the station but we missionaries were getting fewer and rumours were going around that were worrying. We carried on our work as usual but things seemed different. Then, somehow, I don't know how it happened, there was just C and myself at Bongonda—all the other missionaries were gone.

Once a month it was arranged for a doctor to fly in on an MAF plane to have a week operating on any patient in need of surgery. On the Monday morning, the day the doctor was due to arrive, the station would be heaving with people wanting to see him. Those few hours prior to the doctor's arrival were hectic as folk came from far and wide with the hope of getting their problem solved. We were kept busy organising people whom we thought needed to see the doctor more urgently, and when he came later on the Monday morning he would select those whom he would operate on from that group for the five days he would be there. As soon as he had chosen the cases, it was full steam ahead.

The theatre team were flat out, desperately trying to get the packs and instruments sterile ready for the next case, the trained nurses opening up and sewing up each patient. Then the doctor would leave again on the Friday in the MAF plane, leaving us to care for all the patients who had had surgery.

The following week we were up to our necks in newly operated cases, some quite serious and needing lots of special care. We had just a week then, preparing all the things we would need for his next visit. There was linen to repair, holes in gloves to patch, all the packs and instruments to be sterilized, to be as ready as we could be. Then a day or two to relax, and it all started over again!

During the time the doctor was there operating, I didn't get home for a meal until we had finished, going from 7 am till after 8 pm each day. I was exhausted, and each month I struggled to get through. Just at this time, news came through that war had broken out just to the south of us. It was a very difficult time, and for our dear pastor who was so concerned for our welfare.

On the doctor's last visit, just as he was about to get into the land rover to be driven to the airstrip to go to the plane, a lady was carried in by jungle ambulance. They had come a long way. She was skin and bone with the most enormous swollen abdomen that I had ever seen. She was unable to eat anything and was struggling to breathe.

The doctor put his suitcase down, asking for an injection to numb a small area on her abdomen. Also, a suture, a scalpel and a tissue forceps, a prick and a tiny incision and a bit of tissue grabbed, then a tiny hole through the tissue and a drainage tube inserted. 'Drain it very slowly' he said 'no more than (I think he said) a litre in twenty-four hours, and keep going until all the fluid has drained out, then tie the suture and push it back through the tiny incision'—and he was gone. All that as she lay on the contraption on which she had been carried in, which had been laid on the ground at the doctor's feet. I can't remember how much was drained from that ovarian cyst but the dear lady could at last eat again. She was my last patient at Bongonda.

We packed our things, giving away as much as we could, for we were all leaving. The church had decided that we should go.

Why? I never did know why, and just at that time I felt too ill and exhausted to ask or even care. Two missionary men went to close the hospital down and one told of an incident with a laden truck trying to cross the river at Banalia. It was not in the best state of repair and one fault was that the brakes didn't work. After much debate with the men that worked the ferry, an attempt was made to get the truck onto the boat. It freewheeled down the slope and then with much revving of the engine went up the slope and onto the deck. With no brakes, though, it couldn't stop and kept going, much to the delight of the large crowd that had gathered. It sped over the deck and straight into the fast flowing crocodile-infested waters. There was a dead silence until, a few moments later, a head popped up above the water and a very wet figure swam to the bank, only to be arrested by the policeman waiting there. A cheer broke up and several men and boys jumped into the river to see if they could get any of the goods for themselves.

How did this happen?

Caroline brought me home, for which I was most grateful, for I would not have made it on my own. I had been on medication, which ended when I got home. I really felt ill but I couldn't stop, I couldn't rest at all. I cleaned the house from top to bottom and then started at the top again. I couldn't leave the house, not even to go through the door outside. I couldn't sleep day or night and I had to be doing something all the time.

After about a week the doctor came to see Granma, as they did once a month, in those days. When he saw me he said, 'Hello, what are you doing at home?' I explained the situation and he wrote me a prescription for one tablet. 'There, take that, it will do the trick.' Beattie had to go and get it, and it worked! How glad I was that God brought my doctor just at the moment I needed him.

I rested up for a while and then began to consider my future. When God spoke to me at Grange-over-Sands about being a missionary all those years ago, I saw it as a life service, not a few years and then come home and do something else. So staying at home didn't enter into my thinking. It was, 'Where does God want me to go now?' I prayed and sought God's will, 'Lord, where shall I go now?' It was never, 'What now Lord, what do You want me to do?' It never entered my head that God might not want me back in Africa. Wasn't I a missionary for life?

Doctor John and family had gone up-country to a place called Nyankunde where there was a well established hospital, prayed into being by Dr Helen Roseveare and written about so beautifully in her book *Give Me This Mountain*. It was in the Savanna area, not the jungle, and was well established in the hills next to the town of Bunia. There were many more missionaries there, quite a few American and some other nationalities. It was a nurse training hospital and some of the missionaries from our patch had relocated there. So that was where my thoughts centred.

Was that where I should go? Not, is that where God wants me to be? What a big difference there is between the two! What a mistake not to realise that! When I got a letter from the doctor at Nyankunde telling me they could use me, then I was convinced. Silly woman! How Satan as the enemy can come like an angel of light and lead us astray. So, I applied to the Mission again, but they were not too happy. I had returned sick from Bongonda—could I take the pressure? The Mission wanted to test my endurance and I was sent to a hospital nearby on the female medical ward for three months. It was a very heavy ward and the ward sister knew why I was there and piled on the pressure. However, I came through and the Mission was satisfied that I was fit to go to Nyankunde.

So the date was set and I found myself in a totally different environment, one I was not as keen on. The hospital was beautifully situated on a hill and I found myself high up on the hill in the lower half of a property with a family living in the upper part, Edward and Hilde. Ed was doing the accounting and book-work for the hospital and they were with UFM as I was. It was pleasant so high up and I had a lovely view. Happily I settled in and was made very welcome by my fellow missionaries.

Everywhere was fresh and green with lovely flowers. I had a lawn in front of my little home with a border of flowers. A huge mango tree on one side of the lawn provided shade, but as an 8 ft green mamba was found in its branches and killed by my gardener, I thought it best not to shelter under it.

One plant was very special. It grew to about 6 ft, and although rather spindly it had lovely shaped green leaves. The buds started to open early in the morning, giving a hint of the beautiful white flower curled up inside. When it opened in the morning it was like a medium white rose. However, if picked early and kept in the fridge in water, it could be put onto the table when expecting guests for a meal in the evening and it would change to a beautiful deep pink before the meal was over. It was fascinating to watch this happen.

There were no leopards to worry about, but we still had the snakes and tarantulas. The climate was totally different, although there were still the wet and dry times but so different from the jungle area. Severe storms with thunder, lightning and strong winds resulted in a lot of damage, with trees being blown down and roofs flying through the air during the wet season.

The dry season was so very different, though. The day would start lovely with sunshine, pleasantly warm and calm, and as the day went by it got hotter and the wind started to blow, gently at first, but by midday the searing heat, together with the wind, made it feel as if you were in a fan oven. It dried our mouths and noses, cracked our lips and made our eyes red and sore. I didn't like it at all! It was difficult to see, to breathe and to speak.

My work was to oversee the operating theatre and the intensive care unit. Right from the start, however, I was made to feel superfluous by the nurses in ITU and was absolutely ignored by the theatre staff who made it very clear that I was not wanted. In fact, there was only one elderly nurse who would say anything to me at all. I was perplexed and hurt and I couldn't think what I had done or said to upset them.

I mentioned this to the doctor, but he was so busy and he had no problem with them. I'm sure he thought things would settle down. Things didn't get any better, though, they just got worse. It was very clear to me that they didn't want me there and were doing their best to make me leave.

It was a bit better in ITU, but they were doing a good job for the patients in their care and as it was only a six-bed unit there was only so much I could do there. I did complain again about the problem I was having in the theatre unit, but I believe the doctor was doing extra work at the time as another doctor was away, so in all fairness he didn't have too much time to investigate.

It began to take its toll on me as I started to get migraine type headaches which lasted about four days. It got so bad that I seemed to have a headache all the time, as when the four days were up another headache started on the opposite side of my head. I was in terrible pain constantly. I was far from happy.

Why did I not start to question if I was in the place God wanted me to be? It never even crossed my mind. Perhaps it was that God had something else in mind, because one day when the post came I received a letter that surprised and shocked me and I could hardly believe what I was reading.

It was from home. Beattie and Dolly wrote every week without fail, so having a letter from them was not what shocked me. As I read the letter, I could not believe what I was reading. They were coming out to visit me for four weeks. I stared at the letter, not knowing what to think! I was thrilled to think that they would have such a lovely holiday, but I didn't want them to see me like this. But they were coming, flights to Nairobi in Kenya booked! My mind reeled! A thousand things were going through it.

They would, of course, stay with me, but I only had one small bedroom. Well, with a struggle I could put two beds in it, but what about me? Where would I sleep? I did have two of my tin trunks, one on top of the other in the living room, and I could sleep on top of those I supposed, and it could be seating in the daytime. It all began to fall into place and it did, I suppose, take my mind off the situation at work. The headaches, however, didn't get any better.

I booked a flight on the MAF plane to Nairobi and it was arranged that we stay at a hotel until we could get the MAF flight to Nyankunde. The hotel had small, bungalow style, two-bed buildings around a rectangular courtyard. A high wall surrounded it and one could hear ferocious dogs barking nearby. I had arrived in the afternoon and Beattie and Dolly's flight would be due in the next morning.

The vehicle came to pick me up to take me to the airport to collect them. The lady who drove me there came with me, and after a short wait we saw them coming towards us accompanied by a very smart uniformed man carrying a suitcase. I must admit to being a bit anxious when I saw him, wondering what trouble they were in, but he was smiling and so were they. It was the first time either had ever flown, and one was 79 years old and the other 80 years old. They had survived safely in spite of my fears!

The accompanying gentleman was a pilot who had collected them like VIPs from their seats on the plane before the other passengers were allowed to move, I believe. He had taken them through customs etc., collected their luggage and delivered them safely into my hands at the airport exit. Wow! The Lord does things in style.

Our driver took the suitcase, and with one either side of me we went to the vehicle to go to the hotel. We sat and talked for a while and then they went to the next bungalow, but Dolly would not go in. 'Get that out, I am not going in while that's in there,' she said. 'That' was only a poor old lizard, just out to get an evening meal of flying creatures. 'He is harmless,' I said. But no, he had to go.

It was two very excited ladies who got into the transport taking us to the small Wilson Airport in Nairobi to catch the six-seater MAF plane that was to take us to Zaire. Being the smallest, Dolly was put in the tail part, much to her delight, then the rest of us and the luggage; a quick wave to the lady who had transported us, and we were airborne.

Their faces were a picture. What a wonderful view we had, so much better than in a large aircraft. We were able to view the area we were travelling over, picking out little villages, rivers and savannah so much more interesting than jungle. We touched down at Bunia airport to go through the formalities of entering the country, and then back into the plane for the short trip to Nyankunde airstrip, where Doctor John was waiting to welcome us and transport us up the hilly terrain to my little home.

It was two tired but very excited ladies who sat and had a cup of tea that the houseboy had prepared for us. Dinner was a short walk away, up the stairs to the upper apartment where Ed lived with his wife Hilde. Their two children were away at boarding school at the time. Hilde had prepared a lovely meal for us, which we so appreciated. That afternoon they caught up on some lost sleep.

They were made very welcome by all the other missionaries and most days we were invited out for meals. With so many nationalities we had many different ways to get used to. Being invited one day to dinner, our beautifully cooked beef dinner was served to us and we were to help ourselves to vegetables. Also on the table, next to each plate was a bowl of fruit in jelly. No, it wasn't dessert, it was to be eaten with dinner!

Beattie and Dolly

Chapter 21

We visited the hospital and folk greeted them wonderfully. On one ward a little girl was half hiding behind her mum's skirt. Without thinking, Dolly, who adores children, went slowly towards the child, who fled screaming, causing great merriment among her relatives, but great distress to Dolly. Each morning I showed my face at the hospital but spent more time at home than usual.

God uses our mistakes

O n Sunday we went to church and they were just amazed at the numbers that had come to worship. Every available place taken and then everyone shuffled along until not one more could be accommodated on the bench. Folk crowded around the windows and doorways, straining to hear the person speaking. A large crowd gathered around the church building, all hoping to hear the words being spoken. The speakers could make themselves heard quite well even without any amplifying systems. What a joy to see such amazing crowds.

My family were formally welcomed by the pastor. They couldn't understand a word, and as it was in Swahili I wasn't much better. But those who could understand told us of all that was being said. They were amazed and delighted, of course, for they had not expected such a welcome.

When the service was over there were so many who waited patiently to shake them by the hand and welcome them personally. We were a little late going for dinner that day, but our hosts understood as they were there with us and were quite used to African time.

When patients came to the hospital, they always brought a relative or two to care for them and cook meals. There was an area at the back of the hospital designated for this purpose. One afternoon we went to visit these ladies as they were busy preparing a meal for the sick one. Each one had a fire, with three big stones on which the cooking pot was placed and the fire lit beneath it. Some were more advanced with the meal and were already pounding away at the already cooked manioc roots with the green leaves in the pot over the fire to cook.

If more family members came with the sick one, there would be more to help, so two people might be pounding away rhythmically in the same vessel. These vessels were carved from wood, with one part shaped like a basin that had a flat base that sat on the ground. A long pole was used to pound up the cooked food that was put in it, to make the food just how they liked it. Both of these utensils were beautifully carved and decorated. My family were fascinated to see how these dear ladies prepared their food.

When night time came the sick person was on the bed, plus any children they brought with them, or it might be the husband sleeping on the bed, with the patient underneath. It was not always easy to know which one was the patient! As we walked among these friendly ladies who, instead of shaking hands while involved in the meal preparation, always offered their wrist, we could see how much work went into even preparing a meal.

Dolly was so interested in all that was going on that she didn't notice a little girl, about 7 years old, getting closer and closer, always with an eye on Dolly, ready to run for her life if she thought she was noticed. Closer and closer she crept and then, reaching out a tiny hand, she touched Dolly's arm, and then ran her fingers down it, fascinated. Dolly turned her head to look at her and a look of horror came over the child's face. She was too scared to run, but as Dolly's face broke into a welcoming smile and with her own finger gently ran it down the child's arm, she relaxed and looked up in wonder at this white woman, who then held out her hand and took the child's tiny one in hers. The little girl relaxed and walked with Dolly for the rest of the time we spent with them. The look of wonder on the little girl's face was just lovely to behold!

We were invited one afternoon to tea at a Swiss nurse's house, and watched as a storm approached. The sky was black and menacing, the wind getting stronger and stronger, and the rain began to fall, gently at first, then the lightning flashed, and the thunder crashed, making one really scared at what damage it could do—when suddenly, the whole roof of the house opposite took off and sailed through the air until it was out of sight beyond the horizon! There was no calling on any firm to come and replace it, or get quotes etc., or even wait. The man who lived in the property was up there in a very short while, with new roofing and a team of workmen, and it was fixed before nightfall—what service!

While we were at the Swiss nurse's house, she invited us to go with her to visit two single lady missionaries working not too far away. She drove us in her little car and we were able to see a bit of the countryside with small villages dotted here and there. The houses were made differently from those in the jungle, as there were few trees to use. So mud bricks baked in the sun were supplemented and grass was used on the roofs. It was lovely seeing them going about their daily tasks with a cheery wave to us as we passed by.

When we got to the home of the two ladies we were visiting, all three of us were surprised to see how like the African people they lived. They cooked a meal for us—rice and soya beans—a normal meal for them, but we so enjoyed that meal—it was all they had to offer and they shared it with us. It certainly taught me a lesson and I felt rebuked at the way I had unthinkingly lived at Bongonda, way below my usual living standards but way above the living standards of African people around me.

Needing the toilet before we left, they pointed to a block of brick-built loos and gave us a large piece of lovely African cloth saying, 'Take this, you will need it.' We were puzzled by these words, but when we got there we saw why. There was a row of loos but not one with the privacy of a door. They were set up high on a bank, but just a very short distance in front of them was a road with people walking both ways along it, calling out to us, 'Yambo, yambo sarna bamama'—'Hello, hello ladies.' So, two held the material over the door way while we each, as quickly as possible, availed ourselves of the facilities. How glad we were it was not a windy day!

The Swiss nurse also took us another day to visit the Baka people (or pygmies) at the Baka Visitor Centre. It was fascinating to see their homes, their hunting skills, dancing, clothing (or lack of it), the intricate beadwork, preparing the food and cooking. We didn't care to see them smoking and getting high on whatever it was they were inhaling, but we did so appreciate the dancing they did for us and being taken by our dear friend. It was so kind of her to give such enjoyment to my dear folk and me. I was so thrilled that it was in the jungle and they could see the kind of environment I had worked in. They heard the sounds of jungle creatures, birds singing and they saw beautiful blue and also yellow large butterflies with long pieces trailing from their beautifully marked wings, as they all clustered around a damp mud hole, all flying up at once when disturbed.

We watched beautiful groups of tiny birds on the wing, bee eaters I think they were, their lovely mid-blue feathers shimmering against the paler blue of the sky as they feasted on the myriad tiny airborne insects. The lovely hummingbirds, their iridescent feathers shimmering blue or green as they hovered before the flower from which they were extracting the sweet nectar, were also a delight. There were so many precious things to see and tuck into one's memory to recall at a later time of reminiscing. So the days went on all too quickly and then they were in their last week.

One morning the houseboy came to work with a live chicken in his arms. 'This is for Mama,' he said. Beattie and Dolly were overwhelmed that he would give them a gift out of the very little he had, and after the gardener had killed and feathered it, Beattie gutted it and found it was a laying hen! She asked him why he had given his laying hen and was amazed when he replied, 'Only the best for Mama.' (When he later became the proud owner of a lovely wristwatch courtesy of Mama, his joy knew no bounds.)

So the holiday came to an end, and it was time for the homeward journey. We travelled to Nairobi in the six-seater MAF plane again, and stayed over at Mayfield Guest House until the flight next day. All went without a hitch and the pilot was there to take care of them with their luggage. He took them through customs and on to the plane, found their seats for them and stayed with them and saw them settled. He left them just before takeoff and wished them a good flight.

I went back to Mayfield for the night, and then it was on to the MAF plane to return to Nyankunde, just the pilot and myself. It was not a good journey for clouds made it difficult for the pilot to see where he was going.

These planes flew by pilot sight, not by instruments, and he could not see where he was because the weather closed in unexpectedly. He feared we were over Uganda and at that time there was the danger of being shot down, as this is what the Ugandan government had threatened to any plane entering its air space. We went higher to avoid difficulty, but by doing so it was hard to recognise anything so far beneath us.

It got colder and colder the higher up we got and I began to feel very afraid. I was praying to our heavenly Father to protect us and to show the pilot something he would recognise. Shortly after, through a small opening in the cloud, he saw a river and we were not where we ought to be. So he decided to turn back to Nairobi.

As we travelled, I was watching the clouds before us and saw a huge white cloud begin to billow up in front of us, and then I could just make out a black spot in the centre of it. What was it? I couldn't make it out. As I focused on it, it seemed to be getting bigger the nearer we got to it. Then coming closer, I could see what looked like a rainbow encircling the black dot. I had never seen a circular rainbow before. I stared at it, not able to take my eyes away. It was getting bigger as we got closer and I stared, straining my eyes, trying to make out what it was.

Still the pilot was looking this way and that, trying to get his bearings. I continued praying and staring.

As it got that bit nearer, I looked in amazement, for I could just make out in the centre of that rainbow circle what looked like a small plane. In fact, I felt it was the very plane I was travelling in. My heart went out in thankfulness to God, for his promise of protection. I remembered that after God had destroyed the world by flood in the time of Noah, He promised never to flood the earth like that again. He said He would put His bow in the sky as a token of that promise He had made to us. (We can read about this in Genesis 9:12–16.)

I felt He was saying to me at that moment, 'Don't be afraid, my child, you are safe in my arms. I will take care of you. You are encircled by my promises and love.' I relaxed, knowing all would be well.

The many promises God has spoken to us in His Word are bountiful and precious and we can trust every one of them. As I gazed in awe and wonder at the image before me, which was getting bigger and bigger all the time, the fears left me and His peace flooded my heart.

As the colours in the rainbow became brighter, I realised that whatever kind of problem I might face in the future, however hard or difficult, there would always be a promise to meet it, to fit it; all I would need to do was to trust my heavenly Father to deal with it for me.

As I look back now from this vantage point in my life, I realise that God was showing me that there were going to be turbulent times ahead, but that He would be with me through them all. In the many troubles, God's manifold grace and promises would always be sufficient, if I would only put my trust in Him.

To God be all the glory

A short time later we arrived back at Wilson airport and I was taken back to Mayfield Guest House. As there was no available room, I found myself alone for the night in the basement. As I get very claustrophobic, this was the worst thing to happen to me. Let me describe what the basement was like. It was a space under the building, which was supported on several blocks. There were no windows and so no light or ventilation was available. It was a dirt floor with a few beds, I believe, with a table or cupboard to each one.

The lady who ran Mayfield took me down and showed me where the light switch was and left. I began to panic. 'I can't stay down here,' I thought. I sat on the bed and began to pray. As I prayed I grew a little calmer. I remembered how God had reassured me of His loving care and protection that afternoon and words of Scripture tumbled into my mind. 'Fear not, for I am with thee;' 'I will never leave you nor forsake you;' 'I am with you always.' As these precious words crowded into my mind, I calmed down and felt comforted. I switched on my torch and turned off the light, making my way back to my bed for the night. I got in and thanked the Lord for his presence and comfort. 'Thank you for your wonderful promises, Father.' 'I will lay me down and sleep in peace for you only, Lord, make me to dwell in safety' (Psalm 4:8). I switched off the torch, closed my eyes and slept soundly till morning!

There was no MAF plane to Nyankunde that day, but there was the following one. Another night in the basement again! 'Help me again, please, Lord,' I prayed. That night though, I was not in the basement but in a vacant room in the apartment of the lady that ran it. How kind of her to take pity on me. 'Thank you, Lord.' The following day I arrived safely back in my little home in Nyankunde.

Things however, didn't get any better. If anything, they got worse! I was in no fit state to work and two doctors decided I should go home. I was devastated. How had this happened? What was I to do? The door to the mission field was firmly closed. I felt I had failed, let the Lord down.

In those days that I spent packing before my flight home, I spent much time in prayer, seeking the Lord. Several times one particular verse of Scripture stood out and I couldn't ignore it. 'Go home and tell what God has done for you' (Luke 8:39). The first time I turned the page over quickly pretending I had not seen it. However, there it was again, and again and again! Certainly God wanted me to see it. He wanted me to come home! I knew I couldn't fight against God, so reluctantly (not the right attitude at all) I got on with the packing and prepared for the homeward journey with a very sorrowful heart.

During those days a serious accident occurred not far from the hospital, involving an army vehicle. One soldier had been killed and others were in intensive care. As I was still working a little at that time, I went to see them and had the joy of introducing three of them to the Lord Jesus, whom they joyfully welcomed into their hearts as their Lord and Saviour.

So, the day came for me to leave. I was struggling with tears as I boarded the MAF plane to take me to Nairobi, stopping at Bunia for the formalities necessary for leaving the country. It was some weeks later that I heard that Doctor John had gone to Bunia airport to intercept the head nurse who worked in the theatres at Nyankunde. He discovered that this nurse had been making regular flights to the capital Kinshasa with instruments, suture material and anything else used in surgery that he could lay his hands on. I believe that he was intending to set up his own practice one day when he had stolen sufficient for his purposes. At least I now knew why they were all horrible to me. They were afraid I would discover their secret.

It was a very sorrowful journey home, but I hoped the reason for the headaches would be discovered and put right. My family was, of course, very pleased to see me. Life would be much easier for them as I managed to get a little Mini car second-hand so that they were not dependent on others for transport to go to church or for shopping. It was a joy to meet my dear church family again and also meet new ones who had joined since my last visit. I learned, too, of the amazing story of Dolly and Beattie's visit to me just a month or so before.

Let me pause here and share the story with you.

When I travelled to Nyankunde, both Beattie and Dolly came with me to Heathrow airport to wave goodbye and wish me God speed. A person from UFM was also there for the same purpose. During the course of conversation this person asked them if they had ever thought of visiting me while I was abroad. No! It had never crossed their minds that it could be possible. When they got home, they discussed it together, but it seemed extremely unlikely. They couldn't afford the airfare for they were both pensioners: one was 79 and the other 80 years old. They had never been abroad or flown in a plane. No, best forget it, for it was out of the question.

The idea, however, would not go away. They began to pray about it and asked the Lord to show them if it was His will. Lovely verses from God's Word began almost jumping off the page at them, verses like 'Delight thyself also in the Lord, and He shall give Thee the desires of thine heart' (Psalm 37:4) and 'God delights to give good gifts to His children.'

How thrilled they were with such assurances. They also began to save every penny they could and at the end of each week they emptied their purses into a 'Zaire holiday purse.' They were amazed at how the money mounted up. Beattie was a very good cook and could make wonderful meals very cheaply. As the weeks went on, the Zaire holiday purse began to bulge and the day came when two very excited elderly ladies stood on the pavement outside the travel agents, the proud owners of two return tickets to Zaire!

All this time, not a word had they divulged to anyone. They began packing a suitcase ready for the trip and reality began to dawn. The concerns started and the questions: how would they be able to lift this heavy suitcase? How would they get to Heathrow airport? The suitcase was so heavy, they couldn't move it, let alone carry it to the airport. So it was back to prayer. 'Lord, please show us what to do. We have problems that we can't solve, please help us.'

They were so excited about visiting me that somehow it slipped out that they were planning the holiday of a lifetime. So folk knew that they were planning to go, but not a word about any needs or problems they were facing were spoken of. Then offers of help came from different ones. However, they always had an 'if'—'If it's not a weekday, I could take you to the airport,' or, 'If it's not at night, I could take you.'

They went to the Lord in prayer and said, 'Lord, this won't do, please send someone who will be willing to take us, whatever time it is, or whatever day it is.'

A few days later, the phone went and it was Beattie's niece. 'Auntie, Phil says, if you need a lift to the airport, he will take you and bring you back, no matter what time of the day or night' (Phil was Beattie's nephew). They were thrilled. What an answer to prayer!

They went back to the Lord with another request. 'Lord, we have never flown before, so please will you send someone to help us?' A few days later the phone went again. It was the same niece. 'Auntie, we were telling a relative about your trip to Zaire and she has a son who is a pilot with BA and he says that he will meet you at the airport and take you through the formalities and see you on the plane.' Wow! What an answer to prayer! They were getting the message that God had this trip in mind for them. So the days sped by and two very excited ladies stood waiting for P to come to take them to board their flight.

When they arrived at the airport they were met by a very smartly dressed pilot. He introduced himself and took their suitcase from Phil who had picked it up from the room where they had packed it at home. He had taken charge of it until he handed it over to David, the pilot at the airport. Luggage taken care of, it was through the other procedures smoothly and on into the departure lounge before anyone else and onto the plane!

David found their seats and got them each a pillow and a blanket and showed them how to alter the seat to be able to sleep, for it was an overnight flight. He stayed with them until the last minute before the doors closed, telling them that he would be there to meet them off the flight when they returned. What's more, he had asked a friend, another pilot, to meet them off this flight and see them safely into my hands in Kenya! That is exactly what happened. Wow! How God answers prayer!

That was not all, though, for the whole process was repeated for the return journey!

However, what now? I felt lost, in limbo, and so ashamed that I had let the Lord down. At least that was how I had seen it. I didn't want people to see the real me, a failure. I put myself into a box and closed the top to all but one, Dolly, but not even she was allowed totally in. But I knew she would understand. I wanted to hide away and not let people see this awful person.

I had interviews with the Mission and they arranged through my doctor for me to get checked over for the headaches. Nothing was found and it was put down to migraine.

I felt it was caused by my situation. I was struggling to cope with this in a 'respectable way' and a migraine headache seemed as respectable a way as I could find! At the time I didn't know that this was what was happening. Through this difficult time God seemed far away, and because of how I felt I didn't really seek God as I should have done. I thought He would be angry with me. How wrong I was!

My quiet times with God were mechanical. I went through the motions but my eyes were inwardly condemning myself and not seeking Him, not looking to Him as I should have been doing.

Work is what I need, I told myself. I must get a job. Having left the Mission I now had no money coming in. At that time, however, jobs were few and far between and I began to despair of ever finding work again. All I could manage was a few hours at a local care home each week. Looking back, I see now that God didn't want me to get a job, He had something far more wonderful planned for me, but at the time I could not see this at all.

'"My thoughts are not your thoughts, neither are your ways my ways" declares the LORD' (Isaiah 55:8). God's plans were so different from mine. If only I had sought Him for His will in all of this, He would have pointed me in a very different direction. How blind I was to His ways for me at that time. '"I know the plans I have for you" says the LORD, "plans for good and not for evil, to give you a future and a hope"' (Jeremiah 29:11). His way was right under my nose and I could not see it. 'Trust in the Lord with all your heart, in all your ways acknowledge Him, and He shall direct your paths' (Proverbs 3:5,6). His ways are good, right and just and perfect. He knows best, and when we make mistakes He doesn't leave us. He helps us through our situation because He loves us and only desires our highest good. Why did I not see that?

I did get a job as a staff nurse on a very heavy ward at the local hospital, eventually moving into elderly care where I continued until my early retirement. So I was able to care for each one of my family until they were one by one called home to heaven. Granma at 100 years of age, Beattie at 86 years and Dolly at 104 years old, and I was so thankful for health and strength and help to care for each one as they needed my help.

I, at that time, desperately needed help. More and more I was beginning to suffer mentally. I tried to hide my struggles from everyone and cried out to God in desperation. He showed me a book in the bookcase. Where had it come from? The family had denied all knowledge of it. It certainly was not the kind of book any of them would buy. I was puzzled, but picking it up I realised that this would be so helpful in explaining things to me. I turned also to my Bible again, asking God to help me as I sought Him in prayer. I was in inner turmoil, as I knew I had failed to take the pathway God had planned for me, and that way was now closed. What could I do? His word was so helpful and the little book revealed how things in my past were affecting my present. I brought these things to God but still had no peace until one Sunday morning at the communion service. We had all risen to our feet to sing a hymn. I didn't get far for I saw a figure in white standing just to the left of me, by the row of chairs opposite. I stared and God communicated to me, though no words were spoken, that all would be well. I needed just to put my trust in Him. A peace crept into my heart and the fear and anxiety began to melt away. I knew all was well between my Lord and me, and healing took place at that moment.

Perhaps I had made a mistake in going to Nyankunde. I don't know, but God can use our mistakes and bring good out of them. If I had not gone, my dear family, who had been so good, kind and faithful to me, would not have had 'a holiday of a lifetime' as they put it. They so enjoyed it and felt so blessed to have had the opportunity. As the old hymn says, 'God moves in a mysterious way His wonders to perform.' How gracious of the Lord to have led me into service for Him. I can only praise and thank Him for the wonderful privilege of serving Him, my precious Saviour, Lord and Master. To Him be all the glory. God said to me, 'Go home and tell what God has done for you' (Luke 8:39). 'Thank you, Lord for the privilege of doing so, and keeping it all so fresh and clear in my memory,' allowing me, dear reader, the privilege of sharing with you what God has done for me, to the glory of His wonderful name.